Twayne's United States Authors Series

ED!TOR OF THIS VOLUME

Sylvia E. Bowman

Indiana University

William Bradford

TUSAS 317

Of plimoth plantation

And first of ye occasion, and Indusments ther vnto; the which that y may truly vnfould, y must beginne at ye very roote & rise of ye same. the which y shall endeuor to manefest in a plaine stile; with singuler regard vnto ye simple trueth in all things, at least as near as my slender Judgmente can attaine the same.

I Chapter

It is well knowne vnto ye godly, and judicious, how euer since ye first breaking out of ye lighte of ye gospell, in our Honourable Nation of England (which was ye first of nations, whom ye Lord adorned ther with, after ye grosse darknes of popery which had couered & ouerspred ye christian world) what warrs, & oppositions euer since satan hath raised, maintained, and continued against the saincts, from time, to time, in one sorte, or other. Some times by bloody death & cruell torments; other whiles Imprisonments, banishments, & other hard vsages; As being loath his kingdom should goe downe, the trueth preuaile; and ye Churches of god reuerte to their anciente puritie; and recouer, their primatiue order, libertie, & bewtie. But when he could not preuaile by these means, against the maine trueths of ye gospell, but that they began to take rooting in many places; being watered with ye blooud of ye martires, and blesed from heauen with a gracious encrease. He then begane to take him to his anciente stratagemes, vsed of old against the first christians. That when by ye bloody, & barbarous persecutions of ye Heathen Emperours, he could not stoppe, & subuerte the course of ye gospell; but that it speedily ouerspred, with a wounderfull celeritie, the then best known parts of ye world. He then begane to sow errours, heresies, and wounderfull dissentions amongst ye proffessours them selues (working vpon their pride, & ambition, with other corrupte passions; Incidente to all mortall men; yea to ye saints them selues in some measure) By which wofull effects followed; as not only bitter contentions, & hartburnings, schismes, with other horrible confusions. But satan tooke occasion, & aduantage therby to foyst in a number of vile ceremoneys, with many vnprofitable Cannons, & decrees which haue since been as snares, to many poore, & peacable souls, euen to this day. So as in ye anciente times, the persecuti-

The first page of Bradford's *Of Plimmoth Plantation*

WILLIAM BRADFORD

By PERRY D. WESTBROOK

State University of
New York at Albany

TWAYNE PUBLISHERS
A DIVISION OF G. K. HALL & CO., BOSTON

Copyright © 1978 by G. K. Hall & Co.
Published in 1978 by Twayne Publishers,
A Division of G. K. Hall & Co.
All Rights Reserved

Printed on permanent/durable acid-free paper and bound
in the United States of America

First Printing

Library of Congress Cataloging in Publication Data

Westbrook, Perry D.
William Bradford.

(Twayne's United States authors series ; TUSAS 317)
Bibliography: p. 165-68
Includes index.
1. Bradford, William, 1588-1657—Criticism and interpretation.
Ps708.B7Z94   818'.1'09   78-4941
ISBN 0-8057-7243-X

For Arlen

Contents

About the Author

Perry D. Westbrook's chief interest as a university professor of American literature is in the writers of New England. His Columbia University doctoral dissertation, *Acres of Flint: Writers of Rural New England, 1870–1900,* was written under the direction of Henry Steele Commager and Lionel Trilling and was published in 1951. Since then Professor Westbrook has written and published books about Mary Ellen Chase, Mary Wilkins Freeman, and John Burroughs, all in the Twayne United States Authors Series; and he has compiled and published an anthology of New England writings titled *Seacoast and Upland.*

On a more general cultural subject, he has written, with the aid of a Guggenheim Fellowship, *Biography of an Island,* a study of a Maine fishing community, which has gone through two printings. Another of his books, *The Greatness of Man: An Essay on Dostoyevsky and Whitman,* has appeared in two editions — the first with Thomas Yoseloff (A. S. Barnes) and the second with the Fairleigh Dickenson Press. He has, in addition, published five mystery novels and contributed essays to such periodicals as *PMLA, College English, New England Quarterly,* and *Nineteenth-Century Fiction.*

India, that Professor Westbrook has followed in recent years is English-language literature written in India. This interest has resulted in articles and reviews for *The Journal of Commonwealth Literature, World Literature Written in English,* and *Studies in Short Fiction.* His first interest, however, continues to be New England; and he has lately written two lengthy essays on Robert Frost, one in *Frost: Centennial Essays,* edited by Jac Tharpe, and the other in Jac Tharpe's *Frost Centennial Essays, II.*

Preface

Much has been written about William Bradford, Governor of the Colony of New Plymouth during all but five of the years between 1621 and 1657. Historians, antiquarians, *Mayflower* descendants, political scientists, literary scholars, critics, theologians, and a vast variety of sentimentalists have been drawn to a study of Bradford's political and private life. Predictably, a sizable amount of what has been published about him is rubbish; but there is also an impressive body of thoughtful and carefully researched material dealing with him. It is obviously helpful to have the results of so much research to draw from, and many of the interpretive and critical writings serve to stimulate and give direction to one's own efforts. Yet the existence of such quantities of printed matter more or less germane to the subject contributes to problems of selection and causes a latecomer to be hesitant about claiming any originality of his own.

Perhaps the chief claim to uniqueness that this volume can make is that, in keeping with the purposes of the Twayne United States Authors Series, it focuses on William Bradford as an author rather than as a political leader or pioneering colonist and is the first (as of late 1974) book-length study to do so. But having said this, I must immediately backtrack: it is impossible to treat Bradford solely as an author, however remarkable his literary talents and achievements may have been. Bradford's greatest work — the only one that really qualifies as literature — is *Of Plimmoth Plantation,* which E. S. Morgan has described as "the outstanding piece of historical writing produced in the United States before Francis Parkman."[1] This book presents an account of the first twenty-seven years of the Colony of New Plymouth and of the events in England and Holland leading to its settlement. More important, this work reflects the political and, more particularly, the religious beliefs and aspirations of the band of Separatists who sponsored and carried out the colonial venture, and it also indicates the personality of its author. *Of Plimmoth Plantation* is significant ultimately as the expression — recorded by a sensitive and skillful writer — of the ideals and values, and the way of life supported by these, of a small but influential group of English Nonconformists who left their imprint on history for better or worse on both sides of the Atlantic for several centuries after their own lifetimes.

Thus the first five and the eighth chapters — approximately two-thirds — of this study are devoted to *Of Plimmoth Plantation*. Chapter 1, which is largely biographical, takes note of the circumstances of Bradford's life as a boy and young man, and presents from Bradford's own point of view the life and character of the man (William Brewster) who provided him with a father surrogate and served as model of Christian character and a pillar of spiritual strength. The next four chapters are concerned with major subjects and themes developed in *Of Plimmoth Plantation* — the community, the covenanted church, relations with and attitudes toward the Indians, the problem of evil, and God's dealings with his elect. If at times in these chapters the emphasis seems more political, economic, or theological than literary, the reader is reminded that *Of Plimmoth Plantation* is about government, business and trade, and religion; and the book occupies itself with these subjects in its own way from the point of view of its author and the people he led. As for the remaining chapters, they discuss Bradford's lesser prose and his poetry, and briefly review recent scholarship and criticism concerning Bradford as a historian and author.

An explanation should be given as regards the title, *Of Plimmoth Plantation*. In most of its printed editions the book has been assigned the title *History of Plymouth Plantation,* with slight variations, especially in the spelling of Plymouth. The only title that Bradford gave his work was *Of Plim̃oth Plantation,* the line over the *m̃* indicating the doubling of that consonant to make *Plimmoth.* In the text of the manuscript he uses the single or double *m* interchangeably. Worthington C. Ford, the editor of the most scholarly and authoritative edition, has adopted the title *Of Plimmoth Plantation* for the page headings, though on the title page he calls the book *The History of Plymouth Plantation.* In the present study, Bradford's title, *Of Plimmoth Plantation,* will generally be used, although for brevity and variety his book will sometimes be designated as the *History,* a practice common among writers on Bradford.

In regard to quotations in this study, the usual policy has been to draw from the first printed version of a work unless a later version more faithfully reproduces an original manuscript. Thus in quoting from *Mourt's Relation* I have used the first edition (1622); but in quoting from *Of Plimmoth Plantation* I have used Worthington C. Ford's extremely scholarly edition (1912), though there are several earlier editions. The result is that much of the quoted material from Bradford and other writers retains its original spelling, capitalization, and punctuation, with the notable exceptions that some abbreviations have been spelled out and that such typographical practices as the use of *y* for *th* or *u* for *v* have not been retained. In cases where the only published edition of a work has been modernized (e.g., Bradford's third *Dialogue* or some of his poems) that version rather than the manuscript has been drawn from.

PERRY D. WESTBROOK

State University of New York, Albany

Chronology

Unless otherwise indicated, the days of the month are dated in Old Style, but the years are dated in New Style.

1590 William Bradford born, probably in March as his baptism is recorded as occurring on March 19 in Austerfield, Yorkshire, England, to William — a prosperous yeoman — and Alice Hanson Bradford.

1591 Father dies.

1594 Alice Bradford remarries. William sent to live with his grandfather.

1596 Grandfather dies. William again resides with his mother.

1597 Mother dies. William placed under care of his uncles, Robert and Thomas Bradford.

1597– Resides in Austerfield; helps uncles with farm work; prob-
1602 ably attends local grammar school; suffers from a prolonged illness.

1602– Bradford a regular attender at Puritan and Separatist meet-
1607 ings in nearby villages.

1606 Scrooby group is formally organized as a Separatist congregation with Richard Clyfton as pastor and John Robinson as teacher.

1607 First attempt of Scrooby Separatists to flee to Holland.

1608 Second, and successful, attempt to flee to Holland.

1608– Residence of Pilgrim group in Amsterdam; Bradford em-
1609 ployed as a silk-worker

1609 Removal of Pilgrim group from Amsterdam to Leyden, with John Robinson as pastor. Bradford employed as fustian-worker.

1611 Bradford comes of age and inherits family property in England, which he sells, using the money to purchase a house and, probably, a loom; perhaps aids in the acquisition of a church building.

1613 Bradford marries Dorothy May, daughter of an elder of the

Ancient Brethren, an English Separatist group in Amsterdam.

1615 (?) Son John born.

1620 Departure of first immigrants from Delftshaven, July 22; arrival in Southampton, July 27; final departure from Plymouth, September 6; arrival at Provincetown, Cape Cod, November 11; drowning of Bradford's wife, either by falling or jumping from the *Mayflower* in Provincetown Harbor; arrival of *Mayflower* at New Plymouth, December 16.

1621 Death of John Carver, the first governor; election of Bradford as governor, a position he was to hold for all but five years of the remainder of his life. Treaty with Massasoit, chief of the Wampanoags.

1622 *Mourt's Relation,* based on diaries of William Bradford and Edward Winslow, published in London.

1623 Bradford's second marriage, to the widow Alice Carpenter Southworth, who had two sons by her first marriage and who bore Bradford three children.

1625 Pastor John Robinson dies in Leyden.

1627 Bradford and seven other Plymouth leaders, with four London Associates, organized as "Undertakers" to assume colony's debt of 1800 pounds to London "Adventurers."

1630 Warwick Patent for colony of New Plymouth issued in Bradford's name by Council for New England. Bradford begins the "scribled writings" which eventually take form as *Of Plimmoth Plantation.* Arrival of last group of Leyden Brethren to reunite with the Plymouth congregation.

1637 Pequot War.

1641 Bradford surrenders Warwick Patent to freemen of colony.

1642 Outbreak of "wickedness" in colony.

1643 Death of Elder William Brewster.

1648 Bradford writes *A Dialogue or the sume of a Conference between som younge men borne in New England and sundery Ancient men that came out of holland and old England,* copied into Plymouth Church Records by Nathaniel Morton in 1680. First published in 1844.

1650 Bradford apparently ceases work on *Of Plimmoth Plantation,* completing the annal for 1646 and compiling his list of *Mayflower* passengers and their progeny.

1650– Bradford composes a number of didactic and admonitory
1657   poems.

1652   Bradford composes *A Dialogue or ·3ᵈ· Conference
        between some Yonge-men borne in New-England, and some
        Ancient-men, which came out of Holand, and Old Eng-
        land, concerning the Church. And the Govermente therof.*
        Published in 1870. (A second Dialogue has not survived.)

1657   On May 9/19 William Bradford dictates his will and dies on
        the evening of the same day.

1855   Manuscript of Bradford's *Of Plimmoth Plantation,* lost
        since 1776, discovered in the Fulham Palace Library in
        London.

1856   *Of Plimmoth Plantation* published for first time, by the
        Massachusetts Historical Society, Charles Deane, editor.

CHAPTER 1

A Yorkshire Yeoman's Son

WILLIAM Bradford, historian and governor of early Plymouth, was only incidentally a literary man; but his major work, *Of Plimmoth Plantation,* is considered by many critics to be the most remarkable piece of writing produced in seventeenth-century America. This unquestioned masterpiece is the history of the beginnings and the early years of the colony to which its author consecrated his talents and his energy and which probably would not have survived without his leadership. From 1606, when the tiny Pilgrim congregation was formed in England in Scrooby, Nottinghamshire, until his death in America in 1657, Bradford was intimately associated with the persons who shared in launching and preserving this first permanent English settlement north of Virginia. Indeed, he served as governor during almost all of the thirty-seven years after the colony's founding. The story of William Bradford's life and work is, therefore, the story of New Plymouth and its origins in England and Holland.

In *Of Plimmoth Plantation,* Bradford scrupulously avoids dwelling upon circumstances related to his personal life; but he does, of course, record his official acts. He also comments frequently about the religious, political, and social ideals and values which he and the community accepted but which did not always find their way into practice. Though basically and intentionally a public document, *Of Plimmoth Plantation* is also a history of its author's motives, aspirations, and frustrations; for these were identical with those of the community — or he thought they were or should be. This element of the personal in a work that was intended to be entirely impersonal gives *Of Plimmoth Plantation* its charm and its status as literary art. Like many works of literature, it reveals a person, a culture, and an age. In specific terms, it reveals the mind and soul of its author and of a group of religious enthusiasts in their efforts to establish, according to their concepts, an ideal Christian commonwealth in a place and under circumstances utterly foreign to their experience.

I *"These Scribled Writings"*

In 1630 or thereabouts William Bradford started the "scribled writings" which he "peeced up at times of leasure afterward" (I, 14) until, twenty years later, he had completed *Of Plimmoth Plantation* as it exists today.[1] The result was a lengthy account, which, though it was not printed in its original form until after two centuries, was used freely by other historians of New England throughout the colonial period. Bradford would doubtless have approved of this use of his material, but the publication of the manuscript would certainly have pleased him better. Indeed, his stated hope was that others would profit from the story he had to tell. To him, as to most Puritan historians, the writing of history was in the nature of a sacred obligation, for it was the recording of God's providence as it worked itself out in human affairs.

The duty of the Puritan historian resembled that of a preacher: to explain to mankind the inscrutable ways of God, to provide examples of God's displeasure as well as His dissatisfaction with human actions, and to warn against evil and encourage righteousness. As one New England clergyman phrased it, the writers of history are "the Lords *Remembrancers*."[2] As a result of such views, both Plymouth and Massachusetts Bay saw fit to allocate public funds for the writing of histories of their colonies. When Bradford's nephew, Nathaniel Morton, did the job for Plymouth in *New-Englands Memoriall* (1669), large parts of it became little more than a transcript of his deceased uncle's *Of Plimmoth Plantation*.

Bradford, as a Calvinist in theology if not in church polity, was utterly convinced that from the beginning of time God had foreseen and foreordained that a devout band of Separatists from England and Holland would sail across the Atlantic Ocean and establish a purified Christian church in the desolate wilderness of North America. Indeed, God had not only foreseen this event and planned it down to the least detail, but He knew with equal certainty that its consequences would last until the end of time. How, then, could an earnest and God-fearing man refrain from writing down the record of such an undertaking for the future benefit of humanity and, more importantly, for the glory of God Himself? Thus Bradford, despite his activities as governor, trader, farmer, and pillar of the church, found "times of leisure" to write *Of Plimmoth Plantation* — a book which, like the *Aeneid* or Exodus, is ennobled by its author's sense of his own and his people's divinely directed destiny.

If great writing develops from a great theme — or at least from an author's conviction that his theme is great — then Bradford's *History,* whatever faults it may have, meets outstandingly this requirement of greatness. Indeed, the book is totally engrossed in the idea of divine guidance of a people whom God had marked for the task "of laying some good foundation, (or at least to make some way therunto) for the propagating, and advancing the gospell of the Kingdom of Christ in those remote parts of the world; yea, though they should be but even as stepping-stones, unto others for the performing of so great a work" (I, 55).

Naturally, the recording of such an important mission leaves little room for an author's expression of his own purely private joys and sorrows, successes and failures, even though he can express those he shares with the community at large. Thus, though Bradford does frequently use the first-person pronoun, he does so almost invariably in connection with his official actions. Almost always he refers to himself as "the governor" rather than by name; and, in regard to members of his family, his reticence is complete. Even the death of his wife by drowning after she jumped or fell from the *Mayflower* in Provincetown Harbor — the question has never been resolved — goes unrecorded in *Of Plimmoth Plantation* — as does his marriage to Alice Southworth, except in the genealogical appendix of the book.

The dearth of strictly autobiographical detail in *Of Plimmoth Plantation,* especially for the years before 1620, is to some extent an obstacle to a full understanding of Bradford; but research has fortunately unearthed some of the circumstances of his life in England and Holland.

II *Boyhood Years in England*

William Bradford was born in the hamlet of Austerfield, in the West Riding of Yorkshire, England, in March 1589/1590.[3] Both his father, also named William, and his mother, *née* Alice Hanson, were of yeoman stock; and they were members of two of the most prosperous and respected families in the village. Before the son was two years old, his father died and left a landed estate of considerable value. Upon marrying again at the end of three years, Alice Bradford put her son under the care of his paternal grandfather. When two years later the grandfather died, the child returned to live with his mother. Following her death shortly thereafter, he was placed under the guardianship of two uncles, Robert and Thomas Bradford. Now seven years old, he was stricken by what Cotton Mather described as "a long sickness,"[4] which apparently was debilitating rather than incapacitating, for it did not prevent him from taking on some of a farm boy's tasks, including the herding of his uncles' sheep. During this period he also must have attended school in Austerfield or some neighboring village, where he learned at least to read — a rare privilege in those times for one of his class. Among the books with which he seems to have formed an early acquaintance were John Foxe's *Acts and Monuments (Book of Martyrs),* Desiderius Erasmus's *The Praise of Folly,* and, above all, the Geneva Bible — the most popular, though not the official, version of the Scriptures during the reign of Queen Elizabeth.

The established church, of course, held sway in Austerfield, and all the Bradfords were probably regular attenders. But a few miles away at Babworth, just across the border in Nottinghamshire, the local parson, Richard Clyfton, had begun preaching Puritan doctrine. While still only twelve or slightly older, Bradford began to attend Clyfton's meetings, most likely in private homes or out-of-doors. In the words of one biographer, "from that moment, the course of his life was changed."[5] Richard Clyfton, whom Bradford many years later described as "a Grave and fatherly old man,"[6] revealed to the yeoman's son a different and hence more exciting view of life and religion than he would ever have had the opportunity to glimpse in his native village. Endowed, obviously, far beyond the capacities of the average country boy, Bradford seized the chance to escape the wholesome but intellectually and spiritually limited environment into which he had been born; and, from this time onward, he shared in the proscribed religious worship of the Puritans and Separatists, who for some reason abounded in his remote area of England. His zest must have been considerably sharpened by the shocked but unavailing opposition of his uncles, whose reactions, it may be assumed, resembled those of a Vermont farmer who discovers that his son has joined the Communist party.

At a nearby community, Gainsborough, across the River Trent in

Lincolnshire, there was a second group of religious radicals who, like the congregation at Babworth, were still within the established church; but these members were striving to reform it from within on Puritan principles. Such reform, however, soon appeared hopeless; and the Gainsborough congregation, under the pastorship of the Reverend John Smyth, a disenchanted Anglican priest, abandoned the state religion and established itself as a Separatist, or Brownist, church. For a time, apparently, Bradford was a member of this congregation — and he walked the twelve miles from Austerfield each Sabbath day to worship with it.

Soon, perhaps for convenience's sake, a second Separatist group formed ten miles to the north, at Scrooby, which was closer not only to Bradford's home but to the homes of others who had attended the Gainsborough meetings. At Scrooby, the Reverend Richard Clyfton, of Babworth, now a thoroughgoing Separatist, officiated as pastor. The Reverend John Robinson, later the chief spiritual guide of the Pilgrims, served as copastor or, in Calvinistic terminology, as the teacher who was assigned the doctrinal instruction of the flock while the pastor concentrated on exhortation. The Scrooby meetings were held in the local manor house where William Brewster resided as bailiff — a residence which, ironically, was owned by the Archbishop of York. Bradford had now associated himself with the most extreme form of religious dissent in the England of his day.

III *Separatism*

An understanding of the nature of the religious radicalism which these rural congregations, led by their defected Anglican clergymen, were espousing is essential to an understanding of the motivation that sent groups like the Pilgrims to self-imposed foreign exile and eventually to colonies in the New World. The Separatists were much more far-reaching in their reformist demands than were the Puritans in general. The nonseparating Puritans would have been content, or so they avowed, with purifying the Anglican establishment of "popish" ceremonies, rituals, and vestments; with dropping the requirement for the use of the Book of Common Prayer in the churches; and with abolishing the hierarchy of priests, bishops, and archbishops.

As for the form of governance that was to supplant the hierarchy, the nonseparating Puritans split into two groups. One advocated Presbyterian rule, consisting of a national assembly, synods, regional "classes" (governing bodies made up of representatives of churches in a given area), and local congregations under ministers and elders. A second, and more radical, group favored a Congregational polity — which was that adopted by the Separatists — in accordance with which each church would consist of a spontaneously "gathered" assembly of "saints" (those chosen by God for salvation). Such a congregation would exist autonomously: it would elect its own ministers and officers and be subject to no form of jurisdiction from a higher source of human power.

Neither of these groups within the main body of Puritanism advocated the step — tantamount to treason — of total secession from the established church. They constantly reiterated that their purpose was to reform the national religion — albeit drastically — and had no wish to sever its connection with the state. With the Congregationalists especially, committed as they were to local autonomy, this claim might seem specious; but they firmly held to their position — as can be seen in the case of the Congregationalist Puritans of Massachusetts Bay who stubbornly and perhaps even sincerely denied any intention of separating from the Anglican church. It should be emphasized that all Puritans, including the Separatists, found little to complain of in the theology of the Anglicans as set down in its markedly Calvinistic Thirty-nine Articles. Their quarrel was with Anglican polity rather than with doctrine.

But the Separatists, sometimes called the Brownists after Robert Browne, one of the founders of the movement, had the courage — or foolhardiness — to recognize what would seem the logical consequence of Congregational polity — that of complete separation from the national church. With each congregation entirely independent and self-ruling, there would be no conceivable need for any state sponsorship. Since under this dispensation the hierarchy would be abolished and the crown would lose control over religion, both the bishops and the monarch opposed the Brownists more bitterly than they did the main body of Puritans. Thus, in defiance of the church and state, congregations like that at Scrooby were gathered and held their meetings clandestinely at great risk to the worshipers. Eventually, for the sake of the survival of their churches, emigration to Holland became a necessity — a course followed by several Separatist groups in England, including those at Scrooby and Gainsborough.

IV *Young Manhood of William Bradford*

Bradford Smith in his carefully researched biography, *Bradford of Plymouth,* theorizes quite plausibly, in the light of twentieth-century psychology, that Bradford as a boy and an adolescent was seeking a substitute for the father he had so early lost and for the paternal surrogate, his grandfather, with whom he lived after his mother's remarriage but who died when the boy was only six. Twice deprived of a father, and twice deserted by his mother (once when she married and again when she died), Bradford was indeed an orphan; and it is doubtful that the two uncles who took him in charge when he was seven and who, according to Cotton Mather, "devoted him, like his ancestors, unto the affairs of husbandry,"[7] made this sickly and precocious boy feel any less an orphan.

As has been seen, Bradford's early attendance at the Reverend Richard Clyfton's services at Babworth had opened a way of escape from the uninspiring life at Austerfield with its routine of farm chores and its conventional and probably rather mechanical Anglican Sunday worship. Clyfton had had something new to say — something that would appeal to an intelligent youth's imagination and, above all, something that such a youth would grasp at as a rejection of much that was stultifying to mind and soul in his daily life.

But Clyfton was not the only attraction, at least for long. Another was William Brewster — the bailiff of Scrooby and a friend of Clyfton's and John Smyth's — who was an attender at Separatist meetings in the area, who was one of the organizers of the Scrooby congregation, and who was later ruling elder of the English Separatist Church in Leyden and Plymouth. Old enough to be Bradford's father, Brewster was a man of great human warmth as well as of religious zeal. Unquestionably Bradford Smith is correct in stating that it was he "above all others who most influenced Bradford's life."[8] Brewster indeed served not only as father but as teacher, for it undoubtedly was from him, educated as he had been at Cambridge University, that Bradford not only first acquired a taste for learning but also received some practical help in the pursuit of it. Beyond a doubt he had access to Brewster's library, which at Brewster's death in New England numbered over four hundred volumes — phenomenally large for that time — and which, though especially strong in theology, was quite varied in range of subject matter. Brewster, moreover, was a man of the world who had been deeply involved in politics and diplomacy before becoming bailiff of Scrooby. Thus in age, in position in the church, in education, and in breadth of experience, he was a person to be respected by any adolescent or young man in need of a father substitute. After Bradford eventually moved into the Brewster household as a member of the family, he remained there until shortly before his marriage to Dorothy May in 1613.

Yet Bradford's relationship with Brewster was not one of excessive dependence. After the flight to Holland in 1608, Bradford found employment as a silk-worker during the short period at Amsterdam and as a fustian-worker in Leyden, whither the group moved in 1609 to get away from the wranglings of the English Separatists at Amsterdam. In 1611, Bradford, then twenty-one, came into an inheritance of land left by his father. This he converted into cash, which he used wisely and responsibly on such projects as contributing to the purchase of a church, the buying of a loom, and the purchase of a house. His marriage to the daughter of a Separatist residing in Amsterdam was the final step on the road to self-sufficiency and emotional maturation, but there is every reason to believe that his friendship and admiration for Brewster suffered no decline and that he continued active and became increasingly influential in church affairs. Indeed, his election to the governorship of Plymouth in its first year attests to the status he must have enjoyed among his fellow churchmen.

As has already been pointed out, *Of Plimmoth Plantation* only rarely records its author's feelings in connection with purely personal matters. But in dealing with three closely related subjects — the Separatist church, the community of Plymouth, and Elder Brewster — Bradford does not suppress his feelings; and his writing on these includes some of his most moving prose. Not even God, who receives His full share of attention, is treated with greater depth of feeling, perhaps because God to the Puritans was aloof, impersonal, and inscrutable. The very soul of Bradford's *History,* the force that makes parts of it inspired writing, is his deep and undying attachment to the man, the religion, and the people that in his youth gave his life a meaning which it would hardly have acquired in the usual course of an English yeoman's existence. Thus to a very limited extent *Of Plimmoth Plantation* does constitute a spiritual autobiography of the sort so well exemplified by Jonathan Edwards's *Personal Narrative* or by Cotton Mather's *Diary;* but personal soul-searching was not one of Bradford's intentions.

In marking overtones of emotion in *Of Plimmoth Plantation* one need not disregard or underemphasize the immensely greater importance of the work as objective history, nor need one become involved in a psychoanalysis of its author. But if one is to achieve a full appreciation of the book and of the motives and passions — by no means solely Bradford's — that gave rise to the events it records and which generated its finest prose, the subjective dimension must not be neglected. Out of the events of his life Bradford was creating a private myth which coincided with, and helped create, a public myth — that of the divinely sponsored mission of the Pilgrims. And, thanks to the paraphrases and verbatim transcriptions from *Of Plimmoth Plantation* included in Nathaniel Morton's *New Englands Memorial* and in other colonial histories, this myth became embedded in the New England and finally in the general American consciousness as a foundation element in the national self-awareness. Thus was formed a unifying legend that tended to ennoble a history that in some aspects was far from noble. To Bradford, the embodiment of this ennobling legend was Elder Brewster, whom he venerated even more than he did the saintly Pastor Robinson; for Brewster was a living testimony to God's sponsorship of New Plymouth.

V   *Elder Brewster, a Model Separatist*

Bradford's account of William Brewster in *Of Plimmoth Plantation* deserves close attention. Written with meticulous and loving care, it is one of its author's most successful efforts at characterization as well as at a presentation of a model of Puritan piety and virtue. How truly this portrait represents the actual man need not concern one, for what is really important is the light the portraiture casts on Bradford's own character, thought, and ideals.

Indeed, Bradford records many more details of Brewster's life than of his own. His first mention of Brewster by name is at the end of the first chapter, where he is seen along with Clyfton and Robinson as a leader of the Scrooby congregation and as an elder of it after its removal to Leyden. Bradford is at pains to point out that, during the early years at Plymouth, Brewster was for long periods the highest-ranking officer in the church. As ruling elder, in the absence of a pastor, he conducted meetings and preached sermons, but he was forbidden to administer the sacraments of Baptism and

Communion. So highly esteemed was he that the churchpeople considered him an adequate substitute for their beloved John Robinson, who for a time, it was planned, would remain in Holland with that part of the congregation that did not emigrate with the first group but was expected to make the voyage within a year or so. If Robinson had ever arrived in Plymouth, he would have assumed full pastoral care of the reunited groups, which had agreed to consider themselves a single congregation even while separated by the Atlantic Ocean. But Robinson died in 1625 while still in Holland, and Brewster continued as the chief officer of the Pilgrim church until a suitable pastor could be found.

The esteem and the love for Brewster among the people of Plymouth became quite evident in *Of Plimmoth Plantation,* for Bradford was first in the ranks of his admirers. When Brewster died at the age of almost eighty in 1643, Bradford included in his *History* a eulogy of him that is one of the best-known pieces of writing in the book.[9] "I am to begine this year whith that which was a mater of great saddnes and mourning unto them all," writes Bradford. "About the 18· of Aprill dyed their Reve[ren]d Elder, and my dear and loving friend, Mr. William Brewster; a man that had done and suffered much for the Lord Jesus and the gospells sake, and had bore his parte in well and woe with this poore persecuted church above ·36· years..." (II, 342).

Bradford then describes the circumstances of the elder's death. He had not been sick long, and he had been active almost to the last. He died at nine or ten o'clock in the evening like one who falls asleep, "without any pangs or gaspings, and so sweetly departed this life unto a better" (II, 342). Bradford had undoubtedly been present at the dying man's bedside, for the details of the death which are noted with such care would have been of immense significance to him and to any others present. For the manner in which one dies, that final act of crossing from this world to the next, revealed to the Puritan, or to any orthodox Christian, the state of the dying person's soul — whether, in short, he was destined for heaven or for hell. The peacefulness and dignity of Brewster's passing, "without any pangs or gaspings," was the final proof of what the quality of his life would have caused one to expect — that he was one of God's elect bound for salvation.

Bradford follows his description of the death with a battery of quotations from the King James and the Geneva bibles to the effect that one who suffers much in this world for the sake of Christ, as

Brewster had done, may expect ample rewards in heaven. Bradford then proceeds to present a brief account of Brewster's life and accomplishments: his early service in Holland with William Davison, who was assistant to the queen's secretary of state; his part in organizing the church at Scrooby; his activities in Leyden, where he became a printer of religious tracts banned in England; and finally his years at Plymouth, which Bradford dwells upon more at length. He extols Brewster's willingness "to bear his burthen with the rest" (II, 348), sharing in the general hardships — among them the drinking of "nothing but water for many years togeather" (II, 348). He praises Brewster's work in the fields, his preaching twice on the Sabbaths, and his success in bringing souls to God — which Bradford attributes to a "singuler good gift in prayer, both publick and private, in ripping up the hart and conscience before God, in the humble confession of sinne, and begging the mercies of God in Christ for the pardon of the same" (II, 350).

Brewster was a man of "grave and deliberate utterance, of a very cherfull spirite, very sociable and pleasante amongst his friends, of an humble and modest mind, of a peaceable disposition, under vallewing him self and his owne abilities, and some time over valewing others; inoffencive and innocente in his life and conversation..." (II, 350). The list of virtues continues, but for all the fulsomeness of the praise, there is no reason to suspect Bradford of insincerity. He has taken great pains to compile what was to him an accurate record of his friend's life and character. Doubtless this record is as revealing of Bradford as it is of Brewster, for it was written at the termination of a relationship of perhaps forty years' duration[10] — a relationship that began when Bradford was perhaps only twelve years old and that at its inception gave Bradford's life the direction it was henceforth to follow.

CHAPTER 2

Church and Community

*O*F *Plimmoth Plantation,* like any major work of literature, embodies its author's beliefs and values and reflects those of its time and place. It has been pointed out already in this study that Bradford's deepest emotional commitments, aside perhaps from those to his closest family (and about these he reveals nothing), were to his friend and benefactor, William Brewster; to his church; and to the community of Plymouth. The nature of the last two commitments, as personal in their way as that to Brewster, is disclosed in *Of Plimmoth Plantation* along with the spiritual and intellectual bases upon which they rested. Before considering the purely aesthetic excellences of Bradford's great *History,* the reader would do well to explore its meanings and purposes as its author conceived them.

I *"In the Felowship of the Gospell"*

Bradford was involved throughout his life in founding and in maintaining communities, both religious and secular, or, rather, combinations of the two. To him, the highest values were those fostered by closely knit community living. Love, peace, prosperity, and salvation itself were associated in his mind with the idea of a well-ordered society. But for Bradford, as for all English religious nonconformists of his time, the foundation of any workable and worthwhile community was the covenanted church. Throughout the Middle Ages and all through the Reformation, a firmly established religion was deemed the indispensable basis on which a social order had to be built. Anglicans, Roman Catholics, and Puritans agreed upon this point; but, for the dissenters, especially for ones as extreme as the Separatists, the cohesive, unifying function of a church composed of like-minded, earnest believers was doubly important.

28

The central theme, the one that surpasses in importance all others in Bradford's *Of Plimmoth Plantation,* is that of the church and its trials and fortunes and misfortunes in England, Holland, and New England. For always this church found itself in hostile or alien surroundings. In England, it had constantly been threatened with forcible dissolution. In Holland, though tolerated, it labored under the disintegrating influence of differing social values and religious polity. In New England, it existed in continual danger of destruction by natural disaster, such as famine or epidemic; by a potentially hostile native population; or by competing European colonies.

Nor was the danger at Plymouth always from without. In the community's midst were "strangers" — as the Pilgrims called those colonists not belonging to the Separatist church — who frequently were divisive and contentious, and who always constituted a majority of the inhabitants.[1] Even among the "saints" themselves — that is, the members of the Pilgrim congregation — there was dissension from time to time; and occasionally one of the most prominent persons among them, like Isaac Allerton, created havoc by mishandling colony affairs or by outright dishonesty. Finally, the merchant adventurers in England — the chief financial supporters of the plantation — at times behaved more like enemies than friends because of their greedy clamoring for quick profits on their investments. Danger and adversity had held the colonists together in the early years, but the dangers later became less immediate and living conditions improved. Noting also a cooling of the original unifying religious zeal, Bradford eventually came to the conclusion that a dissolution of community spirit was jeopardizing all that had been achieved since the first prayerful gathering of the Scrooby church.

For the gathering of that church had been the great redemptive occasion in Bradford's life. Everything that he and his fellow believers had accomplished afterwards had begun with that event. Referring to the Scrooby congregation and its bold rejection of the forms and governance of the Anglicans, Bradford wrote a generation later: "So many therefore (of these proffessors) as saw the evill of these things (in thes parts,) and whose harts the Lord had touched with heavenly zeale for his trueth; they shooke of this yoake of Antichristian bondage. And as the Lords free people, joyned them selves (by a covenant of the Lord) into a church estate, in the felowship of the Gospell, to walke in all his wayes, made known, or to be made known unto them (according to their best endea[v]ours) whatsoever it should cost them, the Lord assisting them" (I, 20–22).

This paragraph is perhaps the most important one in *Of Plimmoth Plantation,* for it states the theme of the book, points to the nature of the conflict that gives dramatic tension to the narrative, and makes it more than a compilation of factual annals. All but the last sentence of the passage just quoted is a close paraphrase, if not a verbatim statement, of the words of the covenant undertaken by the members of a Separatist congregation. Gathered together and agreed on certain principles of theology and church government, a group of individuals would by this pledge constitute themselves a church — one which would proceed to elect its ministers, elders, and deacons, and then to ordain them. This was the manner in which they were unalterably convinced that the primitive Christian churches were formed, and no other procedure could rightly be substituted. The covenant was the all-important, and the only, foundation upon which a church could stand. Thus in 1608, John Robinson, one of the founders of the Scrooby church, defined a church as follows: "A company of faithful and holy people, with their seed, called by the Word of God into public covenant with Christ and amongst themselves, for mutual fellowship in the use of all the means of God's glory and their salvation."[2] And Robinson added that the covenanting group should be of a size that could conveniently meet in one place for worship.

So important was the covenant considered in 1676 that it was "renewed" by the Plymouth Church by order of the General Court, the colony's legislature. As the parishioners could best remember, the renewed covenant was in "substance" that "which their Fathers entered into at the first gathering of the church [at Scrooby in 1606]."

In the Name of our Lord Jesus Christ and in obedience to his Holy will and divine ordinances.

Wee being by the most wise and good providence of God brought together in this place and desirous to unite ourselves into one congregation or church under the Lord Jesus Christ our Head, that it may be in such sort as becometh all those whom He hath redeemed and sanctifyed to himselfe, wee doe hereby solemnly and religiously (as in his most holy prescence) avouch the Lord Jehovah the only true God to be our God and the God of ours and doe promise and binde ourselves to walke in all our wayes according to the Rule of the Gospel and in all sincere conformity to

His holy ordinances and in mutuall love to and watchfullnesse over one another, depending wholy and only upon the Lord our God to enable us by his grace hereunto.[3]

II *"Love, Peace, and Communion" within the Church-Covenant*

The Scrooby group regarded its covenant with the utmost seriousness, for it went to great pains to abide by its letter and, above all, by its spirit. The group doubtless realized that its own strength, though ultimately derived from God, resided in unity. At any rate, the church members made every effort to avoid controversy among themselves or with others. As a result, they declined on their arrival in Amsterdam in 1608 to unite with either of the two English Separatist churches that were already there because these congregations were involved in quarrels with each other and were split within themselves. Indeed, a major reason, Bradford states, for the removal of the newcomers to Leyden the next year was to insure against their getting embroiled in such very unseemly contentions, though from the point of view of "their outward estates" (I, 38), it would have been more advantageous for them to have remained in Amsterdam.

In Leyden, under the benign pastorship of John Robinson, who was aided by his ruling elder William Brewster, the group from Scrooby lived for many years in remarkable harmony. "And if," Bradford writes, "at any time, any differences arose, or offences broak out (as it cannot be, but some time ther will, even amongst the best of men) they were ever so mete [met] with, and nipt in the head betimes, or otherwise so well composed, as still love, peace, and communion was continued; or els the church purged of those that were incurable and incorrig[i]ble, when, after much patience used, no other means would serve, which seldom came to pass" (I, 42). Among the English nonconformists — who were much given to internal strife — no higher tribute could have been rendered.

Bradford, who dwells at length upon the harmony that obtained in the church at Leyden, cites testimony from the Dutch to the effect that the English had been peace-loving, hard-working, and certainly law-abiding. The English themselves took great pride in the spirit of concord that governed their lives and saw in it one of their greatest strengths, especially when the time came for their emigration to America. Thus, in their application to the Virginia

Company for support of their colonizing effort, John Robinson and William Brewster, listing the qualifications of the future settlers, emphasized the solidarity of the Leyden congregation, bound as it was by a covenant which obliged them to live in harmony with God and one another (I, 76). The implication at the time, of course, was that an investor might rest at ease, knowing that his money was in the keeping of such a group. But Robinson and Brewster meant exactly what they said, and their assurances were apparently well founded.

More will be said later about Bradford's lament in his old age about the decay of this community spirit in the Plymouth town and church. What is significant at this point is that his memory of the past, to which he looked back with fondness, was not merely an old man's distortion of reality — a sentimental feeling that the best is always in the past — but had its origin in historical fact. Invariably, in the years preceding the transatlantic voyage, the chief effort of this particular congregation of Separatists had been to maintain and to establish harmony in terms of the covenant they had sworn to in defiance of the king's officers. On their departure from Leyden, Edward Winslow recalled, their revered John Robinson took special pains to put them "in mind of [their] Church-Covenant."[4]

III   *The Need for a Social Covenant*

A covenant like the one to which the Scrooby congregation subscribed constitutes a powerful basis on which to establish identity — a sense of belonging, of being a part of something very much bigger than any one individual could be. Far from being solely religious, such a bond almost of necessity had to become a social and political force. For example, the Scrooby congregation was English as well as Separatist, and at no time before or after the voyage to America did the members forget their national identity. All Protestant Englishmen in that era were convinced that they were chosen by God to lead mankind in the work of the Reformation, as is made clear in Foxe's *Book of Martyrs.*[5] In the vanguard of this divine mission of the English were the Puritans, including the Separatists.

Thus, much as the English Separatists at Leyden appreciated the tolerance and hospitality of the Dutch, they did not wish to become Dutch — at least in the first decades of their exile, though the process of absorption later became inescapable. A compelling motive for going to America, aside from the threat of renewed war between the Dutch and the Spaniards, was that in Holland the English children were adopting foreign ways — even indulging in frivolity on the Sabbath — or were being so drawn away from the English community that the parents saw that their "posteritie would be in danger to degenerate and be corrupted" (I, 55). Other and related reasons for emigration — much in line with Bradford's thinking and stated by Nathaniel Morton in *New-Englands Memoriall* — were that the offspring, if they remained in Holland, would "lose their interest in the *English* Nation" and that the colonists, despite their bad treatment at the hands of the authorities in England, desired "to enlarge His Majesties Dominions, and to live under their Natural PRINCE."[6] Thus strong was the Leyden group's sense of nationality.

In addition, these inveterate readers of the Old Testament were identifying themselves with the ancient Israelites, the chosen nation of old; and, like the Israelites, they were very conscious of their own race, heritage, and mission. At any rate, Bradford in one of his most lyrical passages mingles nationalism with religious conviction: "May not and ought not the children of these fathers rightly say: Our faithers were English men which came over this great ocean, and were ready to perish in this willdernes, but they cried unto the Lord, and he heard their voyce, and looked on their adversitie. . ." (I, 157–58). In a note to this passage, Bradford himself calls to the attention of his readers that he is echoing Deuteronomy 26:5–7, in the Geneva version: "And thou shalt answer and say before the Lord thy God, a Syrian was my father, who being ready to perish for hungre, went downe into Egypt, and sojourned there with a smale companie, and grewe there unto a nacion great, mighty, and ful of people. . . . But when we cryed unto the Lord God of our fathers, the Lord heard our voyce and looked on our adversitie. . . ."

The actual Separatists on the *Mayflower* — not only those from Scrooby but the much more numerous ones who had joined the group later at Leyden[7] — were convinced that they were in covenant not only among themselves but with God. Unfortunately, however, only a minority (forty percent) of the passengers aboard the *Mayflower* were members of the church, as has already been mentioned. The majority were "strangers" (Myles Standish among them), who had been included in the expedition on the insistence of the London adventurers in order to swell the number of the immigrants and thus increase their chances of survival and profit-making. These were not under the Separatist covenant, nor were they likely prospects for conversion. The need for some sort of restraining document which would embrace the entire party was soon seen to be acute. This need prompted the drawing up and signing of the famous *Mayflower* compact.

Much has been made of the compact as an initial step in the evolution of democratic government in America. Although this document may deserve such acclaim, it was actually intended to be a bulwark against too much democracy — for an alarming spirit of independence was showing itself on board the ship. Some of the "strangers" had learned that the landing was to be made on territory for which no patent (permit) for settlement had been obtained. Reasoning that there would be no firm jurisdiction over the colony either by the Virginia Company or by the Council for New England, they announced their intention to "use their owne libertie" (I, 189) once they were ashore. In other words, anarchy seemed imminent, and the leaders of the "saints" felt an urgent need to curb it at its inception.

Up to this point, the Separatists had lived under such strong governments both in England and in Holland that there had been no need for them to give a thought to the enforcement of civil law. Their church covenant controlled their spiritual lives; their temporal affairs were under the watchful eyes of the civil magistrates. But now they were about to land in a wilderness outside the area in which their patent from the Virginia Company was valid. They would be little better than squatters, and many more than half of their company were unrestrained by religious ties. At this point in the history of the founding of Plymouth Plantation, the church covenant ceased to be sufficient for the planters' needs, and a supplementary covenant became necessary. One was quickly devised and agreed to by "saints" and "strangers" alike.

IV *The* Mayflower *Compact*

The dilemma of the Leyden Separatists in their relationship with the Nonseparatists in their company needs further elucidation. The Pilgrims always zealously adhered to their special identity as a single congregation. In describing their departure from Holland, Bradford emphasized the remarkable sense of shared destiny which this consciousness of identity provided for them: "So they lefte the goodly and pleasante citie, which had been ther resting place near

·12· years; but they knew they were pilgrimes, and looked not
much on those things, but lift up their eyes to the heavens, their
dearest cuntrie, and quieted their spirits" (I, 124). Bradford in this
statement, as in so many of his most lyrical utterances, is paraphrasing the Geneva Bible, specifically Hebrews XI:13–16, which
reads in part:

> All these [Old Testament figures like Noah, Abraham, Sarah, Enoch]
> died in faith, and received not the promises, but sawe them afarre off and
> beleved them, and received them thankfully, and confessed that they were
> strangers and pilgrimes on the earth. For they that say suche things,
> declare plainely that they seke a countrey. And if they had bene mindeful
> of that countrey from whence they came out, they had leasure to have
> returned. But now they desire a better, that is an heavenlie: wherefore God
> is not ashamed of them to be called their God: for he hathe prepared for
> them a citie.

Thus the Leyden congregation members were pilgrims in two
senses: they were pilgrims or travelers in search of a new earthly
habitation; but, more importantly, they were pilgrims in search of
the city of God — exactly as was Christian in Bunyan's *The Pilgrim's Progress,* which was to be written some fifty or so years
later. The biblical metaphor of the two countries — one earthly and
one heavenly — is basic to *Of Plimmoth Plantation,* as will be
made evident later in this study. In the search for the heavenly city,
the church covenant would perhaps have been adequate had it
included every participant in the group committed to the search.
But, since this search had to be conducted in an earthly setting, it
had to involve association with individuals who had no commitment to such a cause. This, indeed, was the predicament of the
Separatists among the *Mayflower* passengers, as they themselves
became increasingly aware during their voyage across the Atlantic,
sharing the cramped decks of the little vessel with many who were
not pilgrims at all in the biblical sense.
     A social — as opposed to a religious — covenant was the most
acceptable solution to these persons who were so prone to thinking
in terms of covenants. The Virginia Company, which controlled the
area to which the Pilgrims had intended to go, had ordered the
leaders of colonizing expeditions in its territories "to make Orders,
Ordinances and Constitutions for the better orderinge and
dyrectinge of their Servants and buisines Provided they be not
Repugnant to the Lawes of England."[8] The Pilgrim leaders fol-

lowed these instructions, but they felt compelled first to ratify them by a formal compact which would summarize all the motives and sanctions for the venture upon which they were embarked — with, however, the exception of the economic motive.

The voyage, the document states, was undertaken "for the glorie of God, and advancemente of the Christian faith, and honour of our king and countrie." In its language, the document paraphrases the church covenant: "[The signers] doe by these presents solemnly and mutually in the presence of God, and one of another, covenant and combine [themselves] togeather into a civill body politick." In words echoing those of the Virginia Company's directive, the compact states that the function of the "body politick" will be to "enacte, constitute, and frame shuch just and equall lawes, ordinances, acts, constitutions, and offices, from time to time, as shall be thought most meete and convenient for the generall good of the Colonie, unto which we promise all due submission and obedience" (I, 191).

The last clause, promising submission and obedience, reflects a universal view during the seventeenth century. Once laws were made and magistrates chosen — both, in the case of Plymouth, by vote of the freemen or their duly elected deputies — submission to them was expected almost as a religious duty. Indeed, the colonists looked upon their magistrates — the governor and his assistants — as stewards of God. This view regarding rulers, whether elected or not, obtained of course in the colony of Massachusetts Bay, as well as in England. No churchman, however nonconformist, would dispute it.

Armed thus with a church covenant for the elect and with a civil covenant for all, the Pilgrims proceeded to choose John Carver as their first governor. Upon his death the following spring, William Bradford was elected in his place; and, with the exception of five years, he served in that capacity until his death in 1657.[9] In other words, for most of the first thirty-seven years of the colony's existence, he was its chief magistrate — God's steward — and was rseponsible for its continuing well-being as a community. And four-fifths of his *History* — that part of it which is in the form of annals — is devoted to his account of his own and his assistants' efforts to maintain Plymouth, both colony and town, as a model Christian community under a religious and a civil covenant. Such was Bradford's purpose in life.

V   *God's Stewards*

Beginning with the events of the latter part of 1621, *Of Plimmoth Plantation* takes on the form of annals — a year-by-year account of what Bradford thought was of significance for posterity to know. It is an impressive record — one in which the author's predominant role, though modestly underemphasized, becomes vividly apparent to the discerning reader. Especially obvious is Bradford's overriding concern with the preservation, at whatever cost, of both a spiritual and a temporal community. The life of the colony depended, of course, on the continuance of a genuinely peaceful political life; for a mere armed truce or an uneasy compromise would not have insured survival. So deeply ingrained in the New England mind was the sense of the necessity for harmonious community conditions that this view outlasted the seventeenth century, when mere survival was so precarious, and continued to be a factor in town politics through the next century and later. Whatever made for discord and strife weakened the defenses of a town embedded in the wilderness and vitiated the quality of life even when the dangers of the wilderness no longer existed.[10]

But to Governor Bradford continuing harmony among the people of Plymouth was of great personal as well as community importance; his own innermost peace of mind was involved. Readers who wish a complete, though perhaps cluttered, picture of Bradford at work on the administrative details of his position should browse through the first three volumes of the *Plymouth Colony Records* and through the first volume of the *Plymouth Town Records*.[11] These official records (parts of the former are written in Bradford's own hand) show him engaged in colony affairs in association with his assistants and with the General Court (the legislature, which sometimes served as a judicial body and which at first was composed of all freemen but later of deputies from the various towns),[12] as well as in town affairs with the Plymouth selectmen and general citizenry. Both as governor and as townsman Bradford led a full life; he served not only as chief executive and as a trial judge but as a servitor of the colony in a hundred different ways — ways that even included providing a bull to service the local cows.

As can be expected, threats to the physical existence of the settlement were numerous and varied; but the most menacing one was the ever-present specter of economic ruin. Lengthy sections in *Of*

Plimmoth Plantation are devoted to Bradford's and the other leaders' efforts to ward off bankruptcy. The financial arrangements with the London adventurers were complicated from the very beginning, and they became even more so as debts piled up and as accounts, always carelessly kept, became more and more confused. Bradford presents minute details regarding these matters, for he wishes to exhibit to posterity the tangle that human weakness and depravity can create. A valuable lesson in the truth of the doctrine of original sin could be learned, he thought, from the business experiences of Plymouth; but the modern reader need not concern himself with these details. The policies that Bradford and his associates adopted to save the honor, the credit, and the existence of the colony are all that need to be considered at this late date because they are of interest primarily as maneuvers in a struggle to salvage what Bradford considered to be a divinely predestined venture.

VI   *Malfunctions in the "Commone Course and Condition"*

The first major adjustment that the governor "with the advise of the cheefest amongest them" (I, 300) made in the interest of harmony as well as of greater productivity was to abolish the communal system of agriculture that had been practiced during the first three years of the colony. Henceforth, instead of working common fields, the harvest from which would go into a common store, each family was assigned a "parcell of land, according to the proportion of their number for that end, only for present use (but made no devission for inheritance), and ranged all boys and youth under some familie" (I, 300). The change was immediately justified by the increased industry of the inhabitants and by the larger acreage planted. Musing on the situation, Bradford concluded that Plato's dream of the blessings of communism was contrary to human nature; for, at Plymouth, the "commone course and condition" (I, 301) had brought only confusion and discontent. The young and strong had been reluctant to expend their energies for other men's families and to have to share with persons who were incapable of hard work. Older men had disliked being counted as the equals of their juniors, and men of status had found it an indignity to be placed on a level with the general populace. Finally, the women had been outraged by having to work for other men's wives.

Bradford himself was fearful lest this leveling might be counter to God's arrangement — one universally accepted at the time — for differences in class and in wealth in human society. If it was objected that the failure of the communal system at Plymouth resulted from selfishness, Bradford answered that, "seeing all men have this corruption in them, God in his wisdome saw another course fiter for them" (I, 303). In other words, Bradford found private enterprise to be the most suitable economic policy for mankind in its fallen state.

Another serious problem faced by the colony first became urgent in 1622 when the London associates sent across the Atlantic a group of colonists "on their perticuler" (I, 325), to use Bradford's term. These colonists were persons who were to be independent of "the generall body" (I, 317) — they were to be exempted from contributing to the common work of the community and to its common stores — but they expected to be fed and cared for at public expense until they could get on their own feet. They "were to have lands assigned them, and be for them selves, yet to be subjecte to the generall Government; which [subjection to the government] caused some diferance and disturbance amongst them..." (I, 317). Also, Bradford writes, "those that come on their perticuler looked for greater matters then they found or could attaine unto, aboute building great houses ... as if they would be great men and rich, all of a sudaine; but they proved castels in the aire" (I, 325–26). In fact, Bradford was amused by their complaints — ones which ranged from "wante of both the sacrements" (I, 363) to the presence of wolves and mosquitoes — that were made by some of these disgruntled colonists upon their return to England and that were later reported to Bradford in a letter from one of London partners.

The presence of these complaining freeloaders, who, if they remained for long, would put a heavy strain on the forthcoming food crop (the first to be harvested since the abolition of the communal system), was disconcerting to the old settlers; and they made their resentment known to the governor. To bring about some sort of stability, Bradford resorted to the time-honored expedient of a covenant — one between the colony and the newcomers. The wording is an example of the forbearance, the mildness, and the general spirit of conciliation which characterized Bradford's leadership and which seem to have been typical of this group of Separatists since their formation at Scrooby.

The first clause states that the colony "doth in all love and frend-

ship receive and imbrace them [the newcomers]; and is to allote
them competente places for habitation within the towne. And
promiseth to shew them all shuch other curtesies as shall be
reasonable..." (I, 326). Other clauses state that the recent arrivals
must obey Plymouth laws and must not trade with Indians until the
termination of the "communallitie" (I, 327). On the other hand,
they were to be "exempte from the generall imployments of the
said company ... excepte commune defense" (I, 326); and each
male over sixteen years old was to be required to pay an annual tax
of a bushel of corn. Certainly the agreement was fair and it seems
to have had the desired effect of preserving a semblance of harmony, but later events proved it to be far from a full solution.

VII   "To Rune a High Course, and of Great Adventure"

In 1627 the London creditors of Plymouth Colony had become
so clamorous and their profits from the fur trade and from fishing
and other activities had proved to be so inadequate that the plantation, under Bradford's leadership, arranged to buy the colony from
the London merchants for the sum of 1800 pounds, which sum was
to be paid in yearly installments of 200 pounds.

The colony was next faced with the ticklish task of dividing the
Plymouth real estate and the other assets which had been held in
partnership with the London "adventurers" and once again the
major consideration was the preservation of peace in the community. A careful plan, the full details of which need not be described,
was devised for the fair division of the land: freemen or heads of
families were to receive shares proportionate to the number of their
dependents, but those whose lots lay close to the town were asked
to "take to them a neigboure or tow, whom they best liked; and
should suffer them to plant corne with them for ·4· years, and
afterwards they might use as much of theirs for as long time, if they
would" (II, 11). Meadowland, of which there was a dearth, was to
continue to be held in common. Livestock and other property were
divided with equal concern for fairness.

Most generous and conciliatory of all, it was decided that recent
comers who had never owned shares in the original company
should be included in the distribution, partly because they too had
borne many of the hardships of colonization but mainly to forestall
any cause for dissension among them. All persons participating in
the division — they were henceforth called "the purchasers" or

"Old-Comers" — would be liable for the debt of 1800 pounds in proportion to the number of shares awarded them. The scheme was carried out with apparent satisfaction to all, and Bradford was able to write that it "gave generally good contente, and setled mens minds" (II, 11-12).

Another victory had been won for community solidarity, but the problem of amassing the funds needed for paying the London debt remained formidable since they would have to be collected from each individual freeman or head of a family — many of whom would be unable or reluctant to contribute their portions. Since this unwieldly arrangement could lead only to dissension among the colonists, it was decided "to rune a high course, and of great adventure" (II, 28) that would expedite payment of the debt. In this arrangement, Bradford and seven "of the cheefe of the place became joyntly bound for the paimente of the 1800 *li.* (in the behalfe of the rest)..." (II, 7), with the proviso that the other colonists would yield to them for six years the full control of the trade with the Indians (the chief source of ready cash available to the colony), including all trade goods and furs already on hand, as well as the use of the several boats normally employed in the trade. The three initiators of this plan were Myles Standish, Bradford, and Isaac Allerton (Brewster's son-in-law, who subsequently swindled the colony). This group took as associates five other Plymouth men — among them Edward Winslow and William Brewster — and four of the former London partners who were to act as agents in England in the selling of furs and in the purchasing of goods for trade.

That the London creditors consented to a plan whereby eight leaders in the colony stood bond for the debt was surely a tribute to the debtors' characters, as Bradford himself in his *Letter Book* states: "For besides our formal bonds, it was our credits and honesty that made our friends [in London] rest and rely upon us, assuring themselves, that if we lived and it was possible, we would see them have their monies."[13] As for debtors, they so desired to safeguard the credit, so flattering to them and so indispensable for the colony's continuing existence, that they — "the undertakers," as the associates were called — assumed the full burden of the debt.

A second reason, which was not confided to the general populace, was "to devise means to help some of their freinds and breethren of Leyden over unto them, who desired so much to come to them, and they [Plymouth people who had formerly lived at

Leyden] desired as much their company" (*History,* II, 28). Indeed, although Bradford regarded the reuniting of the two parts of the Leyden congregation as an obligation which had to be honored, some of the "purchasers" who had no Leyden connections opposed the idea, especially, it may be assumed, since it might cause expense to the colony.[14]

The struggle to pay off the debt and to reach a final settlement with the creditors in London occupied fourteen years, during which period the original six-year agreement between the "undertakers" and the "purchasers" was apparently renewed. The details of the financial problems of these years are complex and relatively uninteresting. The story is one of constant frustration, much of it occasioned by the sharp practices and the flagrant dishonesty of self-seekers like Isaac Allerton; for the Plymouth colonists seemed to impress various rascals as easy marks of confidence schemes of one sort or another. Even the supposedly honest men with whom the planters dealt tended to be shrewd and harsh, for they sometimes levied interest at the rate of fifty percent for necessary loans. Added to all these problems was an appalling incompetence, whether feigned or not, on both sides of the ocean in the keeping of accounts; for the financial difficulties of Plymouth Colony appeared year after year to be beyond solution. Furthermore, efforts to expand the Indian trade into Maine and along the Connecticut River ran head on into competing English and Dutch groups.

VIII   *Plots against the "Saints"*

Bradford and the colony as a whole were plagued not only by unscrupulous businessmen and merchant adventurers: in spite of its remoteness on the desolate edges of the known world, Plymouth seems to have been a crossroads in the wanderings of misfits and eccentrics of many descriptions. Bradford's literary talents are at their most impressive when he undertakes the delineation of character, as was the case in his treatment of William Brewster; but he by no means limited himself to the presentation of Models of Christian living. He is even more effective in depicting some of the persons of dilapidated morality and reputation who drifted through Plymouth or who settled, or squatted, nearby. Though such persons were invariably thorns in the flesh of the Plymouth leadership, Bradford retained a remarkable degree of objectivity and humor in his literary handling of them.

Two of the most colorful of this sort were John Oldham, who had come on the *Anne* in 1623, and John Lyford, who had arrived in 1624. Both were "on their perticuler" and had a considerable following among others of that status. As troublemakers, Oldham and Lyford joined forces and "grew very perverse, and shewed a spirite of great malignancie, drawing as many into faction as they could; were they never so vile or profane..." (I, 382). Lyford, who was an Anglican priest with Puritan but not Separatist leanings, had been sent by the London adventurers, apparently with the idea that he could serve as pastor, and had been described in a letter as "an honeste plaine man, though none of the most eminente and rare" (I, 357). This description was almost entirely misleading, for Lyford proved to be neither honest nor plain; and, though not eminent except in rascality, he was exceedingly rare. He made a startling, even repugnant, impression from the moment he set foot on shore, for "he saluted them with that reverence and humilitie as is seldome to be seen, and indeed made them ashamed, he so bowed and cringed unto them, and would have kissed their hands if they would have suffered him; yea, he wept and shed many tears..." (I, 380). Bradford compares him to Ishmael dissembling tears after he had killed Gedeliah (Jeremiah 41:6). Lyford, as delineated by Bradford, is one of literature's unforgettable characters; and he has frequently been compared to Charles Dickens's Uriah Heap in *David Copperfield*. He was also a major threat not only to the peace of Bradford's beloved community but to the very existence of the covenanted church.

But, despite a bad first impression, the settlers welcomed Lyford with their usual warmth; and Bradford accorded him the customary Puritan deference of consulting with him, an ordained minister, about important affairs of the colony. Lyford in turn joined the church in the approved Separatist manner by making a confession of his faith and by renouncing any former theological errors that he might have held. At the same time John Oldham, who had been a ringleader of discontent "among the perticulers" (I, 381–82), suddenly became affable and apologetic about any trouble, such as writing disgruntled letters to the London partners, that he might have previously caused.

But Oldham and Lyford were soon discovered to be in league with one another, and perhaps with some of the adventurers, to undermine the Plymouth church and government by sowing discontent among the people and sending to England additional letters that disparaged the colony's leadership.[15] Bradford intercepted some of the letters; made copies of the less outrageous ones and, in the case of truly vicious ones, retained the originals; and substituted copies in their place. By this time, Oldham had abandoned his conciliatory posture; for, having been ordered by Myles Standish to take his turn at sentry duty, he had refused; had called Standish disrespectful names; had drawn a knife on him; and, when the governor sought to restore order, had "cald them all treatours, and rebells, and other shuch foul language as I [Bradford] am ashamed to remember" (I, 385). One may imagine the tumult that such an incident would create in a small community like Plymouth. And yet it has its humorous side, for two such egregious rascals as Lyford and Oldham are seldom encountered, and the words Bradford uses in retrospect in his narration of the events indicate that the humor was not lost upon him.

With men like Lyford and Oldham nothing is impossible; no disclosure about them is incredible. After holding a meeting for the purpose of disaffecting the people from the government, they were brought to trial and confronted with their disloyal letters. Lyford "was struck mute" (I, 386), but Oldham, as might be expected, "begane to rage furiously, because they had intercepted and opened his letters, threatening them in very high language, and in a most audacious and mutinous maner stood up and caled upon the people, saying, My maisters, wher is your harts? Now show your courage...; now is the time, if you will doe any thing, I will stand by you" (I, 386–88).

The letters, most of which had been written by Lyford, were indeed distressing to the "saints," for they had been written in a concerted effort not only to subvert the leadership but to thwart the main goals of the colony. Particularly upsetting to Bradford would have been the plotters' purpose to prevent John Robinson and the Leyden congregation from coming to Plymouth, for their presence there was deeply desired by the Plymouth church members for sentimental reasons and as allies in their efforts to curb "the perticulers." Equally galling was the accusation that the church members discriminated against Nonseparatists, that "they utterly sought the ruine of the perticulers" (I, 390), and that they unjustly distributed food. The final outrage was the discovery in one plotter's intercepted letter to England that Lyford and Oldham had planned that Lyford would "minister the sacrements (by his Episcopal caling) without ever speaking a word unto them, either as magistrates or bretheren'' (I, 395).

Both conspirators, as might be expected, were found guilty and banished from the colony. Lyford, on hearing the sentence, "burst out into tears, and confest he feared he was a reprobate, his sinns were so great that he doubted God would not pardon them, he was unsavorie salte..." (I, 396). He avowed in court that he had written lies about the colony. He later made a public confession, again with an outpouring of tears; repented his attempted treachery; and succeeded in putting on so good a show that several of the brethren begged that he be forgiven, so deep and sincere seemed his repentance. However, shortly thereafter he again wrote to England to assert that he had meant all that he had said in his previous letters, which had presumably been delivered either in Bradford's copies or in their original form. This action was too much not only for the magistrates but for Lyford's wife, who feared God might visit some great punishment upon her as well as upon her husband because of his duplicity as well as because of certain unrevealed sins, which she proceeded to disclose.

Lyford, she said, had fathered an illegitimate child by another woman before his marriage; and he had engaged after his marriage in sexual activities with every female servant that might be in the house — and Mrs. Lyford had several times caught him in the act. It was also learned, from other sources, that, while serving in a parish in Ireland, Lyford had seduced a young woman whom one of his parishioners thought of marrying but with whom he wished his pastor to confer to the end that he might advise on the suitability of the union. Bradford warns that he has withheld from the reader some of the "circumstances ... for they would offend chast ears to hear them related, (for though [Lyford] satisfied his lust on her, yet he endea[v]oured to hinder conception)" (I, 417). Lyford's investigation of the girl was thorough enough to enable him to recommend the marriage, which was accordingly solemnized. But the bride soon described to her husband how the minister "had overcome her, and defiled her body..." (I, 417). Confronted by the enraged husband, Lyford found it expedient to leave Ireland.

In the light of these revelations, the Plymouth court experienced no hesitation in carrying out the decree of banishment. With a born storyteller's instinct for rounding out a narrative, Bradford relates how Lyford went to Nantasket to join Oldham, who was already living there. Later he removed to Salem and from there went to Virginia, where he soon died. From sources other than *Of Plimmoth Plantation,* it is learned that he served as pastor in all three places.[16]

Oldham's doings after his banishment were in keeping with his character as depicted by Bradford. In the spring of 1625, the year after he was exiled, he had the gall to return to Plymouth, where he again stirred up trouble by accusing the inhabitants of being traitors and rebels. The authorities jailed him temporarily and then caused him to run a gauntlet in which he was pounded with musket butts — "an honorable passport through a military Bumme-Guard," as the Reverend William Hubbard later described it.[17] Finally, he was placed in a boat which conveyed him from the colony. A year later, on a voyage to Virginia, he was shipwrecked; and, in what he thought were his last moments of life, he confessed his wrongs against the people of Plymouth. He survived, however, and later became reconciled with the Plymouth government, which entrusted him with the custody of Thomas Morton of Merry Mount when that antagonist of the Puritans and Separatists was arrested and sent to England. Finally "Mad Jack," as Thomas Morton called Oldham in *New English Canaan,*[18] was tomahawked by an Indian while on a trading expedition.

Oldham and Lyford were but two of many troublemakers who, Bradford thought, endangered the very existence of the colony. Another was the notorious Samuel Gorton (surprisingly Bradford devotes only one sentence to him), who was banished in 1638 for insubordination or perhaps for fomenting revolt. Yet another evil-doer, from Bradford's point of view, was Thomas Morton, who lived on the edge of Plymouth territory at Merry Mount (or Mount Wollaston), sold guns and ammunition to the Indians, and passed his leisure with his festive companions in drunken revelry and in dalliance with local squaws. Bradford tells the story of the quelling of Morton by Myles Standish, and Morton presents his version in *New English Canaan.* Hawthorne in one of his *Twice-Told Tales,* "The May-Pole of Merry Mount," gives a well-known account of this strange man and his doings.

But the disturbers of the peace of mind of the Plymouth settlers were by no means all outsiders or latecomers to the colony, for some of the worst had been closely associated with the venture from its start. Isaac Allerton betrayed his trust as agent and cheated the colony brazenly by employing its credit and the common funds for his own speculations. Indeed, in one of his transactions he robbed his father-in-law, the venerable Elder Brewster, of two hundred pounds. Equally untrustworthy was Thomas Weston, who was at first an enthusiastic backer of the venture, "a Puritan if not Separatist"[19] himself. Indeed, dissension and attempted betrayal were endemic in the struggling settlement, and the marvel to a modern mind is that Plymouth outlasted these trials.

To Bradford, of course, there was nothing of the marvelous in the survival of the colony; to him, the founding and the perpetuation of it were pivotal in God's plan for the establishment of the true church in the New World. The cohesiveness of the "saints" under any circumstances and any trials was to be expected. The covenant, the cornerstone of community, was destined by heaven to endure, despite periods of apparent weakening yet to come. *Of Plimmoth Plantation* is the history of that covenant, and all the events that Bradford records are shown to have had ultimate bearing on the covenant in its civil and ecclesiastical manifestations. Indeed, Bradford seems to have relished describing the futile attempts of greedy and sometimes anti-Separatist factions on either side of the ocean to intervene in colony affairs. The failure of such efforts only strengthened his conviction that God meant the "saints" to rule Plymouth.

CHAPTER 3

"Saints" and Heathen: Dealings with the Indians

THE chief dangers to the Pilgrim community, both state and church, were internal — moral lapses, dissension, dissatisfaction, and, on occasion, the threat of downright rebellion. Bradford was aware that the colonists were potentially their own worst enemies. The greed, the selfishness, the jealousies of the settlers, even including some of the "saints," were the most threatening and the most subtle menaces to the Pilgrim venture. Yet troublesome outer circumstances did exist. The nearby Dutch and French colonies — not to mention the competing English settlements, like those of Thomas Morton and Thomas Weston on Massachusetts Bay — were unfriendly rivals in trade with several of which armed clashes occurred.

Another major source of worry, of course, was the Indians, an unknown and hence initially extremely frightening presence. Yet during Bradford's lifetime the colony managed to maintain generally friendly relationships with the Wampanoags — the native occupants of the colony's territory — though Plymouth troops did participate in the Pequot War. This maintenance of peace with the Wampanoags was a major triumph of the good sense and the diplomacy which were obviously essential to the survival of the colony.[1]

I The First Indian Encounter

Compared to other sources of possible trouble, the Indians proved quite easy to deal with, for the simplest rules of civilized conduct, combined occasionally with a show of force, were all that was needed not only to avert hostilities but to enlist the aborigines as useful friends and allies. To begin with, Bradford and the other

Pilgrim leaders entertained some very definite preconceptions concerning the Indians as compared with the Europeans. Since the Indians were not Christians, they could be expected to be totally under the sway of original sin and to possess none of the leavening grace that characterized certain individuals in the nations under the rule of the Gospels. Indeed, the Pilgrims had expected worse treatment from the savages because of the numerous accounts of their reputed cruelty that were current in Holland and England.

Because of such reports, prospective immigrants anticipated being in deadly danger from "the salvage people; who are cruell, barbarous, and most trecherous, being most furious in their rage, and merciles wher they overcome; not being contente only to kill, and take away life, but delight to tormente men in the most bloodie manner that may be; fleaing some alive with the shells of fishes, cutting of the members, and joynts of others by peesmeale; and broiling on the coles, eate of the collops of their flesh in their sight whilst they live, with other cruelties horrible to be related" (I, 57). Although no certainty exists about where Bradford discovered these lurid accounts, he and the colonists apparently believed them; and with such expectations they could only be pleasantly surprised by the truth.

The actual facts which Bradford records, with several major omissions, of the Pilgrims' dealings with the Indians make rather tame reading. In the first place, one must realize that the colonists were not enthusiastically expectant, at first, of converting the native Americans, despite Bradford's statement that they had "great hope, and inward zeall ... of laying some good foundation, (or at least to make some way therunto) for the propagating, and advancing the gospell of the kingdom of Christ in those remote parts of the world..." (I, 55). Most of the early missionary work that the English did among the Indians was carried on in Massachusetts Bay through the efforts of persons like John Eliot and the Mayhews of Martha's Vineyard (which was under the jurisdiction of the Bay). Later, some Cape Cod Indians were Christianized by Plymouth clergymen.

The first contacts the Pilgrims had with the aboriginal inhabitants of New England occurred during exploring sorties on Cape Cod while the *Mayflower* was anchored in Provincetown Harbor. On these occasions, the English stole Indian corn, for which they later scrupulously paid the owners; and only one skirmish of little consequence is recorded.

In this instance, the English musket fire must have impressed the natives, for they fled, and their adversaries pursued them long enough to demonstrate a complete disdain for mere arrows. These two episodes — the stealing and later paying for the corn, and the display of aggressiveness in the first armed encounter — set the pattern for most of the Pilgrims' dealings with the Indians during the remainder of Bradford's life. The pattern is interestingly in keeping with the character of the Pilgrims, at least in its earlier manifestations and before the decline in religious zeal; for theirs was a rigid rectitude combined with unyielding firmness — the spirit of the Old Testament, from which, even more than from the Gospels, the Puritans and Separatists derived their morality.

II *Indians as God's Instruments: Squanto, Samoset, Hobbamock*

The pleasant story of the Pilgrims' encounters with Squanto, Hobbamock, and Samoset — the English-speaking Indians who unexpectedly appeared at Plymouth and did so much to help the newcomers get on friendly terms with the local tribe — is known to almost every American school child. Not so well known is the difficulty caused not only by jealousy between Squanto and Hobbamock but by Squanto's plotting to gain power and discredit Massasoit, the chief of the Wampanoags. At any rate, the unexpected appearance of friendly and cooperative Indians in the first months of the colony's existence was regarded by the settlers as an act of God's providence and as a strong indication of His support of the venture. Similarly regarded were the finding of the cache of corn on Cape Cod and the fact that a recent plague had so reduced the native population, including the total extinction of those inhabiting the site of Plymouth itself (their planting fields were used by the settlers), that the danger of serious opposition to settlement was nonexistent.[2] Yet if God had so wrought upon these heathens to induce them to help the settlers, the latter were determined not to misuse their advantage. Every effort was exerted to establish an amicable working relationship. Trade for furs began in the first year, and regular contact was established with Massasoit, who lived at some distance on the border of the present state of Rhode Island and who had visited Plymouth, had been entertained there, and had received a return visit.

As might be expected, in dealing with Massasoit the colonists resorted to their favorite political tool, a covenant, in which it was agreed that neither side would molest the other, that any Indian harming a white man would be sent to Plymouth for trial and punishment, that property stolen from either side would be restored, that the covenanting parties would aid one another in the event of an unjust attack upon either by some third party, that Massasoit should inform his allies of this treaty, and that the Indians, when they came to Plymouth, would not carry bows and arrows. The terms of this agreement, though somewhat biased in favor of the English, were scrupulously observed for over fifty years until they were broken by Massasoit's son, King Philip, just prior to the outbreak of the war named after him.[3]

The colony leaders were so careful about adherence to the spirit of the covenant that they abided by it even in some of their dealings with Indians other than Wampanoags. Thus when three white men were apprehended for murdering a Narraganset, the Plymouth court showed its good faith by trying and executing the murderers, despite the fact that "some of the rude and ignorante sorte murmured that any English should be put to death for the Indeans" (II, 267–68). Some Narragansets who were present at the execution were satisfied that justice had been done. The English were well aware, of course, that expediency as well as justice demanded this punishment, for the murdered man's fellow tribesmen had spoken of a war of revenge. Yet Bradford, at least, seems to have been morally outraged by such murder of the Indians, as he was by other wrongs committed against them. For example, when a group of men sent to the colony by Thomas Weston, one of the London backers of Plymouth, settled on Massachusetts Bay, stole corn from the Indians, and wronged them in other ways, Bradford had no hesitation in castigating his compatriots who had sunk so low; and he expressed his understanding of the anger of the natives. Bradford was well aware that many of the troubles with the Indians, other than the Wampanoags, could be traced to the misbehavior of white men like those in Weston's group.

III *Occasions of Violence in Indian Relations*

On the other hand, in all confrontations with Indian militancy, no matter how justifiable the Indian anger might be, Bradford adhered to that policy of aggressive firmness employed in the first encounter on Cape Cod in the winter of 1620. When the Narragan-

sets during the colony's first summer sent a challenge in the form of
a bundle of arrows wrapped in a snakeskin, the governor "with the
advice of others, sente them a round answere, that if they had
rather have warre then peace, they might begine when they would;
they [the English] had done them no wrong, neither did they fear
them, or should they find them unprovided. And by another
messenger [the colonists] sente the sneake skine back with bulits in
it..." (I, 241).

This kind of quick, decisive action characterized Bradford's on-
going policy of meeting obvious threats from the Indians. This
practice did not stem, however, from his desire to play the bully but
from his consciousness of moral rightness (as he saw it) and of its
favor in the eyes of the Almighty since such treatment suggested the
manner in which the Old Testament Hebrews dealt with potential or
actual enemies. Such a policy was, therefore, an appropriate one
for people who considered themselves to be under the special care
and guidance of God. Nonetheless, this approach sometimes led to
violence; for, if the Indians appeared to be plotting war or to be
harassing the settlers anywhere in New England, the Plymouth
leaders were always ready to exert military force; and they did so no
matter how strong the provocation of Indian hostility might be or
how unjust the English position.

One such military action — this one apparently justifiable — was
directed against the Sachem Corbitant when he threatened the lives
of Squanto and Hobbamock at Namasket, a few miles from Plymouth, "for no other cause but because they were freinds to the
English, and servisable unto them" (I, 225). The two threatened
Indians had apparently been journeying on an errand for the colony and had been waylaid while returning. Hobbamock had
escaped, but Squanto was still being held by Corbitant, and the colonists did not know whether he was dead or alive. "Upon this the
Gove[rno]r taking counsell, it was conceivd not fitt to be borne; for
if they should suffer their freinds and messengers thus to be
wronged, they should have none would cleave to them..."
(I, 225–26).

This dilemma, a typical one, was resolved in the unhesitating
manner that became the rule in such situations. Captain Standish
was dispatched with fourteen men to Namasket, where it was discovered that Squanto had not been killed and had indeed left that
same day. Corbitant denied that he had intended to do more than
to frighten his two captives. Before the facts were made known,

however, Standish's troops had wounded three men, who were forthwith taken to Plymouth for medical care. Here again is an instance of the Pilgrims' combining of firmness with a humanitarian, as well as expedient, concern for the Indians' well-being.

Bradford, who wrote with some satisfaction about this episode, obviously considered it to redound to the credit of the English; but another encounter with the Indians did not end so fortunately. This highly discreditable incident occurred as a result of disgraceful activities on the part of the settlers in the colony founded by Thomas Weston at Wessagusset (in what is now the town of Weymouth) on Massachusetts Bay. Weston's men, reduced finally to near starvation, had stolen food from the Indians; and they in turn were reported to be plotting not only to destroy Weston's wretched settlement but also Plymouth, the inhabitants of which the Indians feared might seek revenge for the massacre of their fellow English.

Warned by Massasoit, the Plymouth colonists again sent out a force under the warlike Standish. This operation must have been distasteful to the Plymouth leaders, for they had nothing but contempt for Weston, their one-time associate, and fully realized that he and his men had brought their troubles on themselves by their own improvidence and reckless ways and by the wrongs they had done the Indians. Yet Plymouth itself was apparently in peril, and besides it would be an unwise precedent to permit the Indians to slaughter white men, even Weston's followers. If the savages were not properly kept in awe, it was thought that the English everywhere in New England would be endangered. The decision as to the strategy to be followed was entrusted to Bradford, Allerton, and Standish (I, 294 n); and they characteristically adopted no half measures.

Bradford in *Of Plimmoth Plantation* does not record the sanguinary details of what Standish perpetrated on this expedition. He merely states that the English "cut of [killed] some few of the cheefe conspirators" (I, 294). When he remarks a few sentences later that he has "touched these things breefly because they have allready been published in printe more at large" (I, 296), his reference is to Edward Winslow's *Good Newes from New England,* which had appeared in 1624 and which had devoted over twenty pages to the expedition to Wessagusset. Also in a recently discovered letter to the London adventurers, Bradford and Isaac Allerton presented on September 8, 1623, a full narrative of what had happened in this punitive action; and they painstakingly attempted to justify it.

According to their account, the Indians, who were treacherous and dangerous, had plotted the destruction not only of Wessagusset but also of Plymouth; and the sternest measures were therefore in order. "We kild seven of the cheife of them," wrote Bradford and Allerton, "and the head of one of them stands still on our forte for a terror unto others. . . ."[4] Although what this message conveyed to the English churchgoers as they beheld it on Sabbath days would be interesting to know, they doubtless were aware of Old Testament precedents and justifications for such actions; but perhaps a few of the Plymouth people had misgivings concerning the deed memorialized by such a grisly trophy. Perhaps, also, Bradford, writing in *Of Plimmoth Plantation* long after the event, had some such qualms about what had been done and less certainty about the necessity of it than when he and Allerton wrote their letter to London.

These qualms may have been Bradford's main reason for not giving a fuller account in his *History,* for elsewhere in it he does not hesitate to repeat material dealt with by Winslow. Fair-minded as he essentially was, Bradford realized that Weston's men had deeply wronged the Indians (*History,* I, 286), and he may well have admitted to himself that — as Worthington Ford has put it — "the course pursued by the Massachusetts Indians was justified by the conduct of Weston's people" (I, 295-96 n).[5] George Willison, in *Saints and Strangers* (1945), also takes the stand that the Pilgrims greatly exaggerated the Indian menace so that they would have a chance to interfere in the affairs of a rival colony and terminate its existence — which was indeed the end result of the action. If such was the case, Bradford might well have had cause for some second thoughts.

IV   *A Chiding from the Reverend John Robinson*

At any rate John Robinson, after learning of the occurrence, took a very dim view of it; for, in a letter written from Leyden and included in Bradford's *History,* the minister severely chided Bradford:

Concerning the killing of those poor Indeans. . ., oh! how happy a thing had it been, if you had converted some, before you had killed any; besides, wher bloud is onc[e] begune to be shed, it is seldome stanched of a long time after. You will say they deserved it [Bradford did emphatically say this in his letter to London]. I grant it; but upon what provocations and invitments by those heathenish Christians? Besides, you, being no magistrates over them, were to consider, not what they deserved, but what you were by necessitie constrained to inflicte. Necessitie of this, espetially of killing so many, (and many more, it seems, they would, if they could,) I see not. Me thinks on [one] or tow [two] principals should have been full enough, according to that approved rule, The punishmente to a few, and the fear to many (I, 367–68).

Robinson proceeds to question whether Captain Standish should not be restrained; for, much as Robinson loves and respects him, he fears "ther may be wanting [in Standish] that tendernes of the life of man (made after Gods image) which is meete. It is also a thing more glorious in mens eyes, then pleasing in gods, or conveniente for Christians, to be a terrour to poore barbarous people..." (I, 369). It is noteworthy that Myles Standish was not a member of the Separatist church. Had he been, his course with the Indians might have been more consonant with the ideal of Christian mercy — or so Robinson might think.

Very likely the account of the affair in Bradford's and Allerton's letter of 1623 — so much fuller and more self-justifying than that in *Of Plimmoth Plantation* — is the version that came to John Robinson's attention in Leyden and caused him to convey to Bradford his expression of deep displeasure at this means of dealing with the Indians. At least, the letter in part concerns the Leyden Separatists, to whom the writers warmly allude: "[as] for our freinds in holand we much desired their companie, and have long expected the same ... indeed if they should not come to us, we would not stay [her]e, if we might gaine never so much wellth." Furthermore, in any affairs concerning the colony, the Leyden group was to be regarded "as principalle in the action and they and we to be considered as one body."[6] With this sense of solidarity between the two segments of the congregation, it is little wonder that John Robinson, pastor of both groups, should feel it appropriate and his duty to chide his New England parishioners for what he deemed their wrongdoings.

Robinson's letter is important in a number of ways. First, its inclusion in *Of Plimmoth Plantation* testifies to Bradford's objectivity, which his truncated, one-sided treatment of the Wessagusset expedition in that book might have put in question. Second, it is an early example of the concern of the Pilgrims about the treatment of the American natives at the hands of European colonists. Third, it spells out a theory about punishment that Robinson had already formulated in connection with the disciplining of church members: care had to be taken "that when the punishment comes to one, the fear might reach unto many, which yet wise men in all public executions would have carefully provided for."[7] This principle that was devised for church governance was obviously known to the magistrates of Plymouth, and there is ample evidence that they observed it in civil government and in their dealings with the Indians — except in the Wessagusset and some later cases when their spirit of vengefulness superseded that of justice.

Fourth, Robinson was reminding Bradford, who was still a member of Robinson's church, that the souls of the unconverted are predestinated to hell, so that not only were the slaughtered warriors deprived of life but they were also plunged into eternal torture — a thought horrible beyond words to any true Christian of the period. The question that Robinson is suggesting but not asking outright is, Why are not you Christian Pilgrims in New England spreading the gospel rather than death among those in whose country you have settled unbidden?

Bradford was doubtless given occasion for thought by these words from a man whom since boyhood he had held in the deepest reverence. And just possibly in later years, as he was writing *Of Plimmoth Plantation* and musing on the past, he might have wondered whether the decline in piety and in church solidarity in Plymouth could have been attributable in part to God's disapproval of the affair at Wessagusset. At any rate, neither Robinson's nor anyone else's warnings altered the colonists' immediate policy toward the Indians. Edward Winslow in his *Good Newes from New England* (1624) speaks of an increasingly prevalent opinion that favored the "returning their [the Indians'] malicious and cruel purposes upon their own heads, and causing them to fall into the same pit they had digged for others; though it much grieved us to shed the blood of those whose good we had ever intended and aimed at, as a principal in all our proceedings."[8] A recent Indian massacre of 347 English colonists in Virginia contributed to this hardening of the Pilgrims' attitude.

V   *War with the Pequots*

In the early 1630s, when two English traders, John Oldham (formerly of Plymouth) and a Captain John Stone were murdered by the Pequot Indians, the efforts by Massachusetts Bay colonists to avenge these deaths only exacerbated the situation and more killings of the English resulted. In 1637 the combined colonies of New England and the Narraganset Indians, whom Roger Williams induced to join the English, attacked the Pequot fort at Mystic; and no evidence of Robinson's benevolence existed in Bradford's description of the slaughter that took place there. The English and the Narragansets had

> approached [the fort] with great silence, and surrounded it ... and so assualted [the Pequots] with great courage...; and those that first entered found sharp resistance from the enimie, who both shott at and grapled with them; others rane into their howses, and brought out fire, and sett them one fire, which soone tooke in their matts, and standing close togeather, with the wind, all was quickly on a flame, and therby more were burnte to death then was otherwise slain.... Those that scaped the fire were slaine with the sword; some hewed to peeces, others rune throw with their rapiers..., and very few escaped. It was conceived they thus destroyed about · 400 · at this time. It was a fearful sight to see them thus frying in the fyer, and the streams of blood quenching the same, and horrible was the stinck and sente ther of; but the victory seemed a sweete sacrifice, and they gave the prays thereof to God, who had wrought so wonderfully for them, thus to inclose their enimise in their hands, and give them so speedy a victory over so proud an insulting an enimie (II, 251–52).

Though Bradford was not present at this massacre and must have relied on eyewitness accounts, he seems not to have recognized hell when it was described to him. His obvious jubilation would surely have shocked Pastor Robinson, but he was by then long since dead.

In summary, the Pilgrims' record in their dealings with the Indians during Bradford's lifetime is mixed. In an effort to preserve the community and the church, the Plymouth leaders were forced — or so they thought — to adopt a policy of expediency that was combined, when possible, with Christian mercy; and the resulting practice was comparatively one of some moderation. After all, the establishment of the New Jerusalem was not to be stained by unnecessary bloodshed; but, as has been observed, the New England Christians were strongly oriented to an Old Testament that provided numerous precedents for harsh dealing with the enemies of God's people. The Indians were heathen; and, though it would be preferable to convert them rather than to kill them, their lives could readily be sacrificed if they seemed to stand in the way of the fulfillment of the divine plan for New England. *Of Plimmoth Plantation* contains the first chapter of Anglo-American dealings with and attitudes toward the red men. To Bradford's and the other Separatists' credit, it is a less sanguinary chapter than many subsequent ones; but their actions also contained the seeds of much future grief and terror.

CHAPTER 4

"Patience against the Evil Day"

I   "The Malice of Satan and Mans Corruption"

FOR reasons that deserve close attention, Governor Bradford was undismayed by the many and varied threats to his colony from within and without. To begin with, he and the more pious among the planters were Calvinists to the core in their theology and were therefore stanch believers in the doctrine of original sin. To a Rousseauean, to a Transcendentalist, or to any other person convinced of the basic goodness of mankind rather than of its corruption, the apparent malice of persons like Oldham and Lyford, not to mention the duplicity of Allerton, would be shocking and depressing. But to Bradford, who was completely convinced about humanity's fallen state, the existence of such sinners was cause for neither surprise nor melancholy. Their presence in a community was even to be tolerated to a certain point — as indeed it was — but they were not to be permitted to wreck the plans and the lives of the righteous. Bradford in his account of Oldham's and Lyford's doings exhibited a strong capacity for objectivity and, more strikingly, seemed to take pleasure in presenting the sheer rascality of his subjects. Although something almost Chaucerian resides in his amusement at, and lack of morbid depression about, the spectacle of human aberration, he did not fail to deplore the sinful level to which some of his associates and fellow colonists were sinking.

Notice has already been taken of Bradford's acceptance of the fact that the communal system was not working: human beings, even the "saints," were just too corrupt to put forth their best efforts for the common good; selfishness was too deeply ingrained in their fallen natures. Bradford had found warnings in the Bible as to what to expect of the mere human; and, on one occasion when there were more than the usual difficulties with the rather rapacious and misunderstanding London merchants, he quoted an appropriate biblical verse with his own wry interpolation: "Psa. 118.8. It is better to trust in the Lord, then to have confidence in man. And Psa. 146. Put not your trust in Princes (much less in marchants) nor in the sone of man, for ther is no help in them [him]. v.5" (I, 258).

John Robinson, the first and most beloved of all the spiritual mentors of the Pilgrims, wrote in a letter in 1620 to the departing members of his congregation: "Woe be unto the world for offences, for though it be necessarie (considering the malice of Satan and mans corruption) that offences come, yet woe unto the man or woman either by whom offence cometh, sayeth Christ, Mat. 18.7" (I, 131). In the same letter, which seems to establish the policy of compassion that was leavened with that strictness that marked the many years of Bradford's administration, Robinson exhorted the colonists to be tolerant of one another's frailties, not only because it is the part of a Christian to be so, but because it is politically expedient.

Yet there had to be firm control, and this control had to be in the hands of the magistrates, who, once elected, had to be obeyed; for, even though they might be of humble origin and status, these officials represented "the image of the Lords power and authoritie" (I, 134). Robinson's insistence upon the power of the civil magistrates and upon the honor and obedience due them was, as already noted, completely in line with seventeenth-century political thought. Even when wrong, the magistrates had to be obeyed, for their authority derived from God, whether they held it by election, by appointment, or by birth.

There is every evidence that Bradford, during his thirty-one years as governor of Plymouth, honored Robinson's recommendations; but at time is was difficult to do so. Robinson had warned: "Store up . . . patience against the evill day, without which we take offence at the Lord him selfe in his holy and just works" (I, 132). One time of such difficulty occured in Plymouth in 1642 when not only several refractory individuals had to be dealt with, but the whole colony seemed to be infected with wickedness, despite the fact, as Bradford points out, that the strictest watch was maintained over the morals of the settlers and that severe punishments were meted out to offenders. Among the evils that surfaced were drunkenness, fornication, adultery, and buggery. Bradford shuddered to name such abominations and trembled "at the consideration of our corrupte natures, which are so hardly bridled, subdued, and mortified; nay cannot by any other means but the powerful worke and grace of Gods spirite" (II, 309).

But the magistrates did not rely solely on God's grace to right matters; they were aware that their duty was to do their human best to stamp out evil. Fines were levied, and the stocks were frequently used to punish drunkenness. Punishments for fornication and adultery were especially severe, including whipping and the wearing of the letters AD for the latter crime. One case of bestiality that had occurred in Duxbury just north of Plymouth not only fascinated but also horrified Bradford. Although he made his usual protestation that he would spare the reader the particulars about such matters, he described the case in considerable detail. A youth of "about ·16· or ·17· years of age [had been] ... detected of buggery (and indicted for the same) with a mare, a cow, tow goats, five sheep, ·2· calves, and a turkey" (II, 328). According to the biblical law — "And if a man lie with a beast, he shall surely be put to death: and ye shall slay the beast" (Leviticus 20:15) — this amazing youth was executed, but not until the animals he had defiled had been killed before his eyes. It could not be complained that the magistrates were not doing their part as God's allies in keeping Satan's works within bounds.

Bradford speculated long and seriously about the reasons for the high incidence of manifestations of original sin in the infant colony. To begin with, he found a covering principle in the Gospel statement that, "wher the Lord begins to sow good seed, ther the envious man will endeavore to sow tares" (II, 329). Perhaps, too, the Devil found this community where a purified religion had taken root to be an especially attractive target for his efforts. Or — and here Bradford demonstrates some acuity as a psychologist — the rigid depression of vice in Plymouth might have caused an outbreak of it to be unusually violent. Then, also, a chronic shortage of workers in the colony had made it possible for undesirable persons to find a welcome there and had set up a tide of immigration that shippers, all too eager to accept the passage money of any one able to pay, regardless of his or her character, did much to encourage. Furthermore, many persons of questionable morality were sent overseas by friends or relatives either in the hope that they would mend their ways in the new environment, or with the desire simply to be rid of them. In general, as Plymouth became more prosperous materially, it became more attractive to settlers; and, like the people of ancient Israel coming out of Egypt, the newcomers were thus a "mixed multitud ... Exod 12.38" (II, 330). The ultimate result, Bradford lamented, was that "by one means or other, in ·20· years time, it is a question whether the greater part be not growne the worser?" (II, 330).

II   *Weakening of the Church*

Fully as serious, to Bradford, as the general corruption and moral collapse among the inhabitants was the weakening of the Plymouth church and of community ties as a result of the dispersal of the population to localities remote from the original settlement. Partly to blame was the scarcity of arable land at Plymouth itself; for, to the present day, that section of southeastern Massachusetts is poorly suited to agriculture. On the other hand, the Plymouth colonists were by background generally more adept in farming than in fishing, in which, though the catch normally was remarkably good on the New England coast, they almost invariably found themselves inadequate. In Bradford's words, fishing was "a thing fatall to this plantation" (I, 353). However, with the migration of Puritans by the thousands into Massachusetts Bay in the 1630s, there was a great demand for grain and for livestock, especially for cows, which the Plymouth farmers sold to the newcomers at exorbitantly inflated prices. Consequently, Bradford reports that "no man now thought he could live, except he had catle and a great deale of ground to keep them .... By which means they were scattered all over the bay, quickly, and the towne, in which they lived compactly till now, was left very thine and in a short time allmost desolate" (II, 152).

During the earliest years of the colony, the settlers had necessarily clustered together to protect themselves from possibly hostile Indians and to combine their labors for the common good — an arrangement that was also advantageous in keeping the church strong and unified. What distressed Bradford most about the dispersal was the adverse effect it had on the church, which to him was the nucleus and the *raison d'être* of the community. Those who had moved across the bay to Duxbury found it inconvenient to attend meetings in Plymouth and thus made the request, which was reluctantly granted, that they be permitted to gather a church of their own. Since no effective way could be found to keep others from scattering, Bradford gloomily predicted "the ruine of New-England, at least of the churches of God ther," and he feared "the Lords displeasure against them" (II, 153).

At one time, in fact, the future of Plymouth town appeared so bleak because of depopulation and a decline in the price of farm products after the few boom years that the townspeople very seriously considered deserting that site and reestablishing themselves at Nauset on Cape Cod (II, 368). In the end, when a few actually did remove to Nauset, Plymouth was further depopulated. What again saddened Bradford above all else was the plight of the church, which he compared to "an anciente mother, growne old, and forsaken of her children. . . . Her anciente members being most of them worne away by death; and these of later time being like children translated into other families, and she like a widow left only to trust in God. Thus she that had made many rich became her selfe poore" (II, 369).

The Plymouth church suffered from other troubles besides the dispersal of many of its members. If the utter seriousness and piety of its congregation are considered, an irony appears in the fact that, during the first nine years in America, it had no settled minister. Its first pastor upon its being gathered at Scrooby was Richard Clyfton, who was succeeded in Leyden by John Robinson — both men who enjoyed the deepest affection and esteem of the congregation. That part of the congregation that emigrated to New England looked forward, of course, to the early arrival of Robinson with the remainder of the Leyden brethren, and for a time no effort was made to find and ordain another man. William Brewster, as has been seen, served effectively in the interim as ruling elder; and, though he was later urged to become pastor, he did not consider himself qualified for the position.

For a number of years, whenever a prospective candidate for the pastorship did appear, he was usually found to be incompetent, if not an outright disaster. The turmoil produced by Lyford, sent under the auspices of the London partners to forestall Robinson's coming, has already been described. After Robinson's death in 1624/25, the settlers began searching with greater urgency for a spiritual leader, but they always exercised the greatest caution. In 1628 Isaac Allerton, returning from a business trip to England, brought with him a young man named Rogers (his first name is unknown) to serve as pastor. He was apparently not ordained, however, for it soon became evident "that he was crased in his braine" (II, 58); and he was returned to England the next year at the colony's expense.

In 1629 a stanch Separatist minister, Ralph Smith, who was

trained at Cambridge University and who had recently arrived at Massachusetts Bay, where, it seems, his extreme Separatism was unacceptable to the colonists, moved to Plymouth, where his views were readily approved. He was elected pastor and duly ordained, but his ministry was far from brilliant. Bradford is tactfully silent about Smith's abilities; but, according to the Plymouth Church records, "He proued but a [poor] healp..., being but of very weake prtes...."[1] As a result of such difficulties; Brewster apparently continued to be the mainstay of the church until Roger Williams, the future founder of Rhode Island, was appointed in 1631 as teacher to serve with Smith.

Williams had come to Massachusetts Bay in 1631, but his religious views had not been approved there. Bradford describes him as "a man godly and zealous, having many precious parts, but very unsettled in judgmente" (II, 161). Although Bradford claimed to have benefited from Williams's preaching, as did others in the congregation, the minister's "unsettled judgmente" manifested itself in 1633 in a number of heterodox opinions which bred controversy and threatened division; and, as a result, he left Plymouth for Salem in 1634 and was accompanied by some of his adherents.[2] Later in the following year, another teacher, John Norton, was appointed. He proved to be quite satisfactory but he unfortunately removed within six months to Ipswich.[3] The same year, 1636, Ralph Smith turned in his resignation, "partly by his owne willingnes..., and partly at the desire, and by the perswasion, of others; and the church sought out for some other, having often been disappointed in their hopes and desires heretofore" (II, 236–37).

III *Better Times for Plymouth Church*

But the luck of the Plymouth church was finally about to change; or, as Bradford might have said, patience was about to receive its reward. After unhappy experiences with a conspirator and lecher (Lyford), an insane man (Rogers), an incompetent (Smith), and a man of strong but unstable opinions (Williams), the Pilgrims were finally favored with Mr. John Reyner, "an able and a godly man, and of a meek and humble spirite, sound in the truth, and every way unreproveable in his life and conversation; whom, after some time of triall, they chose for their teacher, the fruits of whose labours they injoyed many years [till 1654] with much comforte, in peace, and good agreemente" (II, 237). The Reverend Mr. Reyner, a Cambridge University graduate, combined in his character and abilities all the qualities that his predecessors had lacked. Bradford saw the hand of God in this satisfying eventuality; the congregation, after years of waiting and trial, had been smiled on.

Yet Reyner's pastorate was not entirely tranquil. The dispersal of the congregation, so deplored by Bradford, was occurring during his tenure; and there was another unfortunate appointment — that of the Reverend Charles Chauncy as teacher, with Reyner henceforth apparently to serve as pastor.[4] "A reverend, godly, and very larned man" (II, 302), Chauncy was highly opinionated, especially on the subject of baptism, which he held to be lawful only when done by total immersion. The congregation as a whole could not agree with this view, but it attempted to compromise by permitting him to submerge any who so wished. But Chauncy was a man of fixed principles — not one to yield an inch — and he departed after three years to take a church at Scituate. Nevertheless, ten additional years of Reyner's peaceful and effective ministry remained. There is no need in this study to follow the fortunes of the church after his departure in 1654 — seven years after the date of the last annal in *Of Plimmoth Plantation* and three years before Bradford's death.

The dangers to the Plymouth colony and its church that are so emphasized and so dwelt upon at such length by Bradford were the human failings — the original sin — of the Pilgrim settlers, of their neighbors both English and native, and of their associates in London. There is something quite medieval in the way Bradford musters in his *History* the seven deadly sins of pride, wrath, envy, lust, gluttony, avarice, and sloth. The Merry Mounters alone illustrated all of these sins and, as Hawthorne perceived, constituted therefore a sort of animated allegory of all that Puritanism abhorred. But, as has been seen, the deadly sins were well represented both in individuals in Plymouth and in the colony as a society; one did not need to travel to Merry Mount to find them.

Lyford and Oldham together would embody four of them — pride, wrath, envy, lust — and Allerton would be only one example of the evils stemming from avarice. Sloth seems to have been one of the failings among the "strangers," and the increasing prevalence of drunkenness and fornication gave witness to the power of gluttony and lust in the community. The desire for land and wealth, which menaced the very existence of Plymouth church, was, of course, a manifestation of avarice and was rife among the "saints" themselves. Thus Bradford's administration of the colony was a constant struggle, now by frontal attacks, now by strategic retreat and compromise, against the continuous threats from within. These problems were the source of the drama in *Of Plimmoth Plantation,* and the study of such conflict becomes a study in human nature and psychology. Theologically, the colony is, in miniature, a study of the worldwide efforts of Satan to undo the work of God.

IV   *"Warning and Admonition"*

To Bradford, as has been seen, the greatest good that mankind could experience was the fellowship of a church that was composed of God's elect. Such a church, as was repeatedly stated in the Acts of the Apostles, in the Epistles of Paul, and elsewhere in the New Testament, had to be a nucleus of love and harmonious order in a world where wrath and disorder were, and are, the general rule. Around such a church, a peaceful civil community should and may be established, even though it might include many persons not members of the church. It must always be remembered that Bradford had first found security and meaning in life when, as scarcely more than a boy, he had been admitted into the fellowship of just such a congregation of the regenerate. His inclusion in the Scrooby church had constituted, in literal theological terms, a rebirth into another and much better life than that of his orphaned childhood with its formalized, unimpassioned secular and religious routines.

Much is heard in the present century of Fundamentalist or Pentecostal sects which emphasize the idea of the rebirth that one must undergo before he can become a true Christian. These sects are quite traditional in this respect: regeneration, conversion, call the transition what one will, has been considered in Protestantism to be the great event in the life of the soul — the prerequisite for membership in the universal church of the saved of all times and places. The true convert — the person who has been reborn in the spirit — is no longer a mere wanderer on the earth; he is, rather, one among an eternally enduring community from which, according to the Calvinistic doctrine of the perseverance of saints, he can never be separated. One who is convinced of his rebirth and who consorts with others of like conviction has placed himself outside the circle of unsanctified living where doubts, fear, loneliness, feelings of alienation, and the like are endemic.

On the contrary, the person convinced of his regeneration becomes a citizen of a spiritual "city" where the ruling forces are Christ's love of the elect and the elect's love of Christ and of one another. Herein lies a measure of security that one must constantly be on guard to protect; for the evils of the other "city," that of the worldly, and that of original sin which is not totally erased even from the souls of the converted, are constant and dire dangers. The life of the reborn, therefore, is not a slothful one; rather, it involves unending struggle to gain the priceless reward of salvation through all eternity. But to the faithful — and all the elect are such — no struggle is too bitter in this cause. Nor do reversals in the battle dismay them or bring them to despair, for despair stems from a lack of faith and belies one's election. "Store up ... patience against the evill day" (I, 132), Robinson had urged the Pilgrims. God's chosen ones will eventually triumph, if not in this world, then in the next.

Thus Bradford and others among the Plymouth church members had unceasingly before their eyes a purpose whose rightness and whose worth was, to them, beyond question; and the achievement of this goal necessitated the perpetuation of not only the church but of the fragile civil community. But, in addition to this commitment to an all-engrossing purpose, Bradford and perhaps others had an attachment to the community as an early substitute for father and family — an attachment that was profound and quite separate from the religious involvement, though the two fortified each other. It has been suggested that in his old age, as he watched the disintegration of the once-united Plymouth church and town, Bradford did succumb to despair, contrary to Robinson's admonition; but there is ample evidence that such was not the case.

Until the very end of Bradford's life he was firm in his theological beliefs, as may be seen in the two dialogues that are considered later in this study. Bradford, as has been observed, did feel a poignant sadness at the scattering of the Pilgrim church, which he compared to a widow deserted by her children, and he deplored the fact that the colony was plagued by outbreaks of immorality. Yet no evidence exists that he actually despaired in anything approaching the literal sense of the term. The real state of his feelings in the face of an apparent decline in the quality of Plymouth life may be gauged from a passage that he penned in his old age as a note on a statement written by John Robinson and William Brewster in a letter to Sir Edwin Sandys, treasurer of the Virginia Company,[5] during the negotiations for a patent for the settling in America. The writers of the letter had stated, in describing the Leyden congregation, that "We are knite togeather as a body in a most stricte and sacred bond and covenante of the Lord, of the violation whereof we make great conscience, and by vertue wherof we doe hould our selves straitly tied to all care of each others good. . ." (I, 76).

Bradford's comment on this statement appears on a blank page opposite its place in *Of Plimmoth Plantation:*

O sacred bond, whilst inviollably preserved! how sweete and precious were the fruits that flowed from the same! but when this fidelity decayed, then their ruine approached. O that these anciente members had not dyed, or been dissipated, (if it had been the will of God) or els that this holy care and constante faithfullnes had still lived, and remained with those that survived, and were in times afterwards added unto them. But (alass) that subtill serpente hath slylie wound in him selfe under faire pretences of necessitie and the like, to untwiste these sacred bonds and tyes, and as it were insensibly by degrees to dissolve, or in great measure to weaken, the same. I have been happy, in my first times, to see, and with much comforte to injoye, the blessed fruits of this sweete communion, but it is now a parte of my miserie in old age, to find and feele the decay and wante therof (in a great measure), and with greefe and sorrow of hart to lamente and bewaile the same. And for others warning and admonnition, and my owne humiliation, doe I hear note the same (I, 76).

Since this passage, one of the most lyrical in *Of Plimmoth Plantation,* is susceptible to many different interpretations, it demands close attention in any effort to understand Bradford and his book. The simplest, and perhaps the most nearly true, remark that can be made about it is that it is a lament for the past — an old man's dream of what seemed like the better days of his young manhood — a view that is very much in the spirit of that age-old elegiac tradition in English verse that includes the probably seventh-century "Widsith," Alfred Lord Tennyson's "Ulysses," and John Steinbeck's "The Leader of the People." A far-wanderer of advanced age looks back on his years of great adventure, accomplishment, and comradeship of fellow adventurers.

But there is more than this closely knit relationship in Bradford's lament. Not only have most of the old comrades of the Leyden congregation died or been scattered — by God's will, Bradford carefully adds — but in a later generation the bonds of community, already broken, have not been renewed; and this is the work of Satan, "that subtill serpente," who has provided the specious reasons for the breaking of the old ties (not completely, be it noted, "but in a great measure"). Here is cause for lamentation and sorrow, but not for despair or abandonment of future effort. Indeed, Bradford registers in the last sentence of his lament a warning and takes upon himself part of the blame for the situation he deplores. Additional effort may bear more permanent fruit, or so Bradford seems to be saying, when he sounds a call for a return to the old spirit which had achieved so much while it had lasted. For the time being, God for reasons of His own, including perhaps punishment for sins committed, has allowed Satan to gain the upper hand among the colonists. A renewal of the Separatist covenant is very likely all that is needed to regain God's favor. Bradford would have learned from his favorite book, Foxe's *Acts and Monuments,* that periods of adversity like that of even Queen Mary's reign did not mean that God had deserted His elect.

Thus rather than despairing and dismissing the happy past as unrecoverable, Bradford, as should be expected, sounds a call, an "admonition," for a return to faith and brotherhood; for those ways are the best, the only sure ones, as *Of Plimmoth Plantation* was written to demonstrate. To Bradford, the inner condition of men and women is what ultimately counts in the lives of individuals and the communities they form. Outer circumstance — the vast ocean to be crossed, the fierce North American winters, the wild beasts and savages in the forest — need not be feared, even if they bring death, by souls that are armed with faith in God and with the righteousness of their own cause.

CHAPTER 5

Predestinated History

I The Duties of the Historian

PERRY Miller has written that "the entire purpose of the New England historians, of Bradford, Johnson, Hubbard, Gookin, Winthrop, and the Mathers," was "to chronicle the providence of God in the settlement of New England."[1] This statement is somewhat of an exaggeration, at least as it is applied to Bradford and probably to the others as well. At the end of Chapter VI of *Of Plimmoth Plantation,* Bradford explicitly states three incentives for writing his *History:* that the Pilgrims' "children may see with what difficulties their fathers wrastled ... and how God brought them along notwithstanding all their weaknesses.... As allso that some use may be made hereof [of the *History*] in after times by others in shuch like waightie imployments..." (I, 120). To reveal the workings of God's providence is thus only one — though perhaps the most important — of three purposes for which Bradford wrote his book.

As Kenneth Murdock has pointed out, the Puritans concurred in the high esteem in which books of history were generally held during the Renaissance, and he quotes Ben Jonson's apostrophe to history as "the Mistresse of Mans life," "Times witnesse, herald of Antiquitie, The Light of Truth, and life of Memorie."[2] The Renaissance produced a number of outstanding histories — Sir Walter Raleigh's *History of the World* (1614); *The Magdeburg Centuries* (1559–1574), an account of the first thirteen centuries of the Christian religion); and John Foxe's *The Acts and Monuments of the Church* (English Version 1563), commonly known as *The Book of Martyrs.* And, of course, ancient historians like Plutarch, Livy, and Tacitus also commanded close and admiring attention and served as models for Renaissance historians.

This enthusiasm for history obtained among Anglicans as well as nonconformists, and for the same reasons. The nonconformists may have been the more interested of the two groups in the providential significance of history, but not to the exclusion of other aspects. Furthermore, the English colonists, of whatever religious persuasion, hoped that the histories of their settlements might induce others to join them. As a result, colonial history served an additional purpose, one that today would be considered as promoting favorable public relations. Since the colonies wished to attract persons of good character — which in New England would mean people of strong Christian conviction — the colonial historians had still another reason to emphasize episodes and conditions that would suggest divine backing of the enterprises they were describing. Such emphasis was common in these promotional histories, but much more space was actually given to matters of trade, agriculture, defense, and government than to descriptions of religious practices or to speculations as to God's purposes.

In fact, even the most conspicuously "providential" of the Puritan histories — for example, Edward Johnson's *The Wonder-Working Providence of Sions Saviour in New England* (1654) or Cotton Mather's *Magnalia Christi Americana* (1702) — were not solely records of remarkable providences, however intensely the focus may have been upon them. Moreover, the earlier histories were somewhat less confined to reports of God's wonder-working than were those written a bit later. The first settlers were so completely convinced of God's approval and abetment of their projects, and they were so busy carrying out their human roles in His service, that they did not need to call attention with underlinings and exclamation points to God's tokens of His approval. A generation or so later, a decline in religious zeal, combined with less precarious living conditions, prompted the historians, as well as the clergy, to dwell upon the sacrifices and accomplishments of the fathers and, above all, to provide evidence of the divine backing of these achievements. Obviously this purpose was one that was behind Bradford's writing *Of Plimmoth Plantation,* for a falling off in piety and self-sacrifice was all too apparent during the two decades before his death — the period in which he composed most of his book. But, to repeat, this objective was not his sole motive; for, as one commentator has observed, Puritan historians like Bradford "show us piety functioning uncertainly but faithfully in the world along with other motives."[3]

II *"God Is English"*

The more naive historians, like Morton and Johnson, seemed to have regarded God as serving the same function as the United States cavalry in a typical old-time Western movie: whenever the "saints" got into a predicament of the Devil's making, God intervened at the last moment to save His favorites from destruction. Although certain historians or commentators on history from early Christian times onward had truly regarded history as a record of the struggle between Jehovah and Satan, the general idea had its roots in the Book of Deuteronomy, which presents God as aiding His chosen people, the Israelites, under the leadership of Moses in their struggles against their enemies. According to this concept, so long as God's people abided by their covenant with Him, they could depend upon His aid; for they were His instruments in fulfilling His plans for their world.

This so-called Deuteronomic Formula[4] was adopted by two very early Christian historians, Eusebius Pamphili (c. 260–c. 340) and Socrates Scholasticus (fifth century); and it was applied to the history of the Christians, who were thought to have supplanted the Israelites as the chosen people. Bradford, a wide reader in church history, knew the works of both these men, and he found them congenial to his own thinking. But more important in Bradford's formulating a concept of history was Foxe's *Acts and Monuments,* which, though it deals with the whole history of Christianity in England, focuses primarily on the persecution of the Protestants during the reign of Queen Mary. Writing after Elizabeth's accession to the throne, Foxe regarded England as the main scene of the struggle by God's people, specifically the English, to establish a true church. As one critic puts it, Foxe transferred the Deuteronomic Formula to England, which had long considered itself marked by God for his particular attention.[5] Thus in these ancient and modern writings Bradford found a pattern for his own treatment of that important and farthest-advanced phase of God's work in which the Separatists were engaged. "God is English," wrote John Aylmer, one of Foxe's collaborators in writing the Latin version of *Acts and Monuments.*[6]

But, of all early New England histories, Bradford's is broadest in its purposes. True, it contains numerous references to divine providences, but at no time — as will be seen — does its author denigrate the importance of human effort, courage, and resourcefulness. In other words, men are not to act counter to providence but in conjunction with it — actually as part of it. To appreciate this distinctive feature of Bradford's *History,* one need only compare it with the more conventional and commonplace *New Englands Memoriall,* compiled by Bradford's nephew, Nathaniel Morton, from his uncle's manuscript. Morton in places transcribed *Of Plimmoth Plantation* verbatim and elsewhere closely paraphrased it. Its only distinction — a dubious one — is its belaboring, in added passages and frequently in marginal notes, of the providential theme, which Bradford had far from neglected but which Morton thought needed greater emphasis. Yet Morton's book is restrained, in this respect, when compared with Edward Johnson's *Wonder-Working Providence.*[7]

III *History and Theology: God's Plan for the Universe*

Such was the tradition of historiography in which Bradford wrote *Of Plimmoth Plantation,* but of equal importance in understanding his work is a knowledge of the theological doctrines — other than the Deuteronomic Formula — that underlay his interpretation and his handling of events. Much has been said about God's relationship to history and nations, but the actors in history are men and women, and a nation consists of the sum of all its individual inhabitants. God's way of dealing with individuals is in fact even more the subject of theology than is His disposition of whole peoples. In their own lives,Christians of all sects are first concerned with their personal standing and relationship with God. The sacraments involve individuals; the individual may address God directly in prayer; and each person, if Protestant, must spend his life trying to answer the greatest of all questions: whether he is one of the elect or one of the reprobates.

Calvinistic Protestantism, of which the Separatists were a branch theologically (though only partly so in church polity), is preeminently directed toward the individual and his relationship with God and with society; and it demands a constant self-examination on the part of one striving to live according to religious and societal concepts. The influence and presence of this aspect of Calvinism in Bradford's work must be reckoned with, but such consideration has to recognize that he often applies to God's relationship with communities the same theology that more normally is employed to explain God's relationship to persons. Moreover, one must always remember that Bradford saw history in terms of the actions of good and evil individuals. To him, Brewster, Robinson, Winslow, and other unnamed "saints" are the good, the elect, the doers of God's work; Lyford, Thomas Morton, Oldham, Allerton are the enemies, the reprobates.

"Man m[a]y purpose, but God doth dispose" (I, 444), wrote Bradford concerning the sudden death in London in 1626 of Deacon Robert Cushman, a stanch supporter of the Pilgrim colony. This adage, which is traceable to the Old Testament — "A man's heart deviseth his way; but the Lord directeth his steps" (Proverbs 16:9) — succinctly states the main premise of the Puritan view of history and of the lives of individual persons; and this attitude informs *Of Plimmoth Plantation* from beginning to end. It deserves, therefore, further examination as an aid in understanding Bradford and his work.

"God doth dispose" is a fundamental belief of all Christians, but it was especially strong in early Protestantism, in which God is considered all-powerful, all-knowing. Whatever occurs in the world God has known would happen, has intended to happen, since the beginning of time, and hence it must happen. In the Middle Ages, a systematic scheme had been worked out in explanation of God's *disposal* of human and natural events. The explanation was somewhat as follows: God has devised a plan, which is providence, for all places, all persons, and all time. This plan is executed by destiny — which Chaucer calls God's "ministre general" — which in turn manifests itself in, or delegates its powers to, such categories as luck, fortune, the general laws of nature, the angels, even Satan and lesser demons and witches. No force, no power, no phenomena that exist are exempt from the control of destiny; for all contribute, under the supervision of destiny, to the fulfillment of God's master plan (providence) for His universe. But, because the mere human intellect is incapable of grasping this plan in its complex entirety, many events may appear to be meaningless, matters of mere chance, of good or bad luck; or they may appear so to the faithless since the faithful know that nothing can happen to anyone at any time or place without the knowledge and the approval of God.

Such was the foundation concept of God and providence that the Puritans inherited from the Middle Ages and earlier and which they found corroborated in the thoughts of Protestant theologians, like those of Calvin on God's eternal decrees—though the Protestants stripped the theory of the complicating concept of God's delegating His power to destiny and of destiny's delegating it's functions to chance, the angels, nature, and so on. Yet, despite the omnipotence and omniscience of God and the finality of His providence, human beings, in Puritan thinking, were still responsible for their actions and for the results of their actions. Otherwise, as men like Augustine and Calvin saw, human beings would sink into a state of total passivity, believing that nothing that they could do would be of avail to their own or other's lots on earth and in the hereafter.

A sentence or two from the Confession of Faith drawn up by the Westminster Assembly of Divines in 1646 as a distillation of Puritan thought of the previous seventy-five or more years is illuminating: "God from all eternity did by the most wise and holy counsel of his own will, freely and unchangeably ordain whatsoever comes to pass; yet so as thereby neither is God the author of sin; nor is violence offered to the will of the creatures, nor is the liberty or contingency of second causes taken away, but rather established. Although God knows whatsoever may or can come to pass, upon all supposed conditions; yet hath he not decreed anything because he foresaw it as future, or as that which would come to pass, upon such conditions."[8]

In other words, God's unalterable will and plan for the universe through all time and His consequent foreknowledge of the step-by-step working out of this plan down to the smallest detail did not deprive human beings of free choice in their actions and of consequent moral responsibility for them. If the modern reader has trouble in reconciling these two premises, so did many a would-be Protestant Christian of the Reformation and later; for the apparent contradictions in this area of Protestant theology — derived, in fact, from St. Augustine of Hippo — caused more backsliding and apostasy than any other doctrinal difficulty. Yet acceptance of precisely these teachings was among the requisites for membership in churches of the Puritan sects.

IV *Theology and History: The Elect and the Reprobates*

Entertaining such beliefs, a writer like Bradford would of necessity credit God for the occurrences recorded in his history, and Bradford gives such credit in close to one hundred instances. These seem to be direct, utterly unpredictable divine interventions, but they are usually susceptible to one of two interpretations: as signs of God's favor, or as signs of His disfavor. There are numerous examples of each in *Of Plimmoth Plantation*.

Before citing some of them, however, it would be well to examine briefly another Calvinistic doctrine adhered to by Puritan churches — the doctrine of election and reprobation — and the special significance it had for a Separatist congregation. The Westminster Confession of faith states this doctrine succinctly and accurately: "By the decree of God, for the manifestation of his glory, some men and angels are predestinated unto everlasting life [the elect], and others foreordained to everlasting death [the reprobates]. These angels and men, thus predestinated and foreordained, are particularly and unchangeably designed; and their number is so certain and definite that it cannot be either increased or diminished."[9]

Those chosen for salvation pass through some form of religious experience, or conversion, which may be taken as rather certain evidence of their being among the elect. They then undergo a spiritual regeneration or change known as sanctification, which makes them fit instruments for God's use in carrying out His purposes; or, in other words, they become sufficiently freed from the corruption of original sin to be able to will that which is pleasing to God. Such persons may expect from time to time to be vouchsafed signs of God's favor in the form of direct divine intervention in the course of the events that shape their lives — what today most would call "strokes of good luck." The reprobates, on the other hand, may expect strokes of bad luck; or, to put it another way, a person or group that constantly meets misfortune may well entertain grave doubts as to being among the elect.

In most Calvinistic sects, the congregations were composed of a mixture of the elect and the reprobates; and communion was made available to all because, as Calvin himself stated, it would be impossible to separate the two groups, especially as it was generally believed that the reprobates far outnumbered the elect. But the Congregationalists, who included the Plymouth settlers and the Massachusetts Bay Puritans, differed from Calvin because they attempted to segregate the elect from the reprobates; they admitted to church membership, which included the privilege of partaking of the Lord's Supper, only those who presented convincing evidence of being regenerate; but the unregenerate were compelled to attend the Sabbath services. Thus a Congregationalist group like the Pilgrims could claim to be God's people — and Bradford refers to them as such. Such a group could hope for, if not count on, exactly those signs of God's favor in the form of direct and helpful intervention in their affairs as an elect individual could expect; and to a group those tokens would have the same reassuring significance as to an individual.

Of course, neither a community nor an individual could expect complete good fortune, for even the elect might backslide a bit — though, once one was genuinely converted, he always remained so, and needed only to be brought back into line in the event he had transgressed. Also some misfortunes might be visited even on the most piously faithful for their spiritual improvement. Furthermore, it was the belief of many, including Bradford, that the Devil had gone underground in England after the accession of Queen Elizabeth and was effecting his ends by stirring up dissension among the reforming sects. Dissension, indeed, did occur even among the several Separatist congregations in Holland, as Bradford sadly notes. And of course individuals who were supposedly but apparently not genuinely converted could and did suddenly become corrupt and thus injurious to the cause of true religion, presumably through Satan's wiles.

V *"Spetiall Providences"*

Many simple but more or less isolated unexpected providential occurrences beneficial to the Pilgrims are recorded in *Of Plimmoth Plantation,* and these Bradford usually called "spetiall providences." For example, directly after the *Mayflower* arrived at Cape Cod, a scouting party came upon the already-mentioned cache of Indian corn — "a spetiall providence of God, and a great mercie to this poore people, that hear they gott seed to plant them corne the next year or els they might have starved..." (I, 167). Somewhat later on Cape Cod in the first encounter between the English and the Indians, "it pleased God ... by his spetiall providence so to dispose that not any one of them [the English] were either hurte, or hitt, though their arrows came close by..." (I, 171-72) — a divine intervention suggestive of the instances in Homer's *Iliad* in which a god or a goddess protects a favorite by deflecting a weapon aimed at him.

It is noteworthy that "spetiall providences" were of frequent occurrence in the first contacts with the Indians, perhaps because the English had had no previous experiences to draw from. Whatever good fortune befell them would have to be attributed to God rather than to their own sagacity. Thus the friendly Squanto, who appeared at Plymouth out of nowhere and showed the newcomers

how to plant corn, was described as "a spetiall instrument sent of
God for their good beyond their expectation" (I, 202). That
Squanto later died in an apparent state of grace, "desiring the
gov[erno]r to pray for him, that he might go to the Englishmens
God in heaven..." (I, 283), would further identify him as an
"instrument of God." And Bradford attributes to the restraining
hand of the Lord the fact that the infant colony was not overrun by
hordes of savages.

But, of course, Indians were not always involved in these providential happenings. The arrival of a ship from Virginia carrying
much-needed trading goods, though expensively priced, was "another providence of God" (I, 276), as was the coming to them in
1636 of their first satisfactory pastor, the Reverend John Reyner.
However, many other "spetiall providences" took the form of the
punishment of sinners or the retribution for acts unbecoming to
Christians. A famous one involves a sailor on the *Mayflower* who
cursed and reviled the seasick passengers and expressed the hope
that he would "help to cast halfe of them over board before they
came to their jurneys end.... But it pl[e]ased God before they
came halfe seas over, to smite this yong man with a greeveous
disease, of which he dyed in a desperate manner, and so was him
selfe the first that was throwne overbord" (I, 149).

To Bradford, this instance was simply another "spetiall worke of
Gods providence" (I, 149). It could equally well be called a judgment, and as such Bradford regarded another instance in which the
greater number of a shipload of backsliding Separatists, the rem-
nants of the congregation of the contentious Ancient Brethren of
Amsterdam, died of "flux," overcrowding, and lack of water on a
voyage to America. Though Bradford expresses the hope that the
souls of these erring brethren who "brought so great dishonour to
God, scandall to the trueth, and outward ruine to them selves in
this world ... are now at rest ... in the heavens, and that they are
arrived in the Haven of hapiness..." (I, 90–92), he very clearly
implies that their disaster might have been God's punishment for
their unseemly wrangles and questionable way of life, especially for
the sycophancy and dissimulation of their leader, a certain Francis
Blackwell, in winning the Archbishop of Canterbury's support and
blessing for the venture. Bradford wrily concludes that, "if shuch
events follow the b[isho]ps blessing, happie are they that misse the
same; it is much better to keepe a good conscience and have the
Lords blessing..." (I, 92).

At times it is difficult, for Bradford at least, to determine whether or not some seemingly providential event is a judgment. An interesting example of this uncertainty involves two ships sent by the London merchant adventurers "on their owne acounte" (I, 433) — for their own profit — rather than for that of the colony as a whole. One of these vessels was bound for France, where its cargo of fish would command top prices. But, owing to a threat of war between France and England, the ship had to dock in an English port where prices were much lower. The second ship, loaded with furs of great value, was seized by Turkish pirates in the English Channel. Bradford laconically remarks that, to some, these losses appeared to be "a hand of God [against the adventurers] for their too greate exaction of the poore plantation, but God's judgments are unscerchable, neither dare I be bould therwith..." (I, 436).

In the above case, which involved the planters' business partners, Bradford was naturally hesitant to state categorically that God's wrath had been incurred. He was similarly hesitant when shipwreck ended two successive attempts of the Massachusetts Bay colonists to send goods to some of their number who had settled on the Connecticut River. The Plymouth traders, who had previously established posts on the river, resented this intrusion into territory that they claimed providence had intended for their use. The affair became somewhat ludicrous when the Massachusetts Puritans countered, with appropriate biblical reference, that providence had also led them to inhabit this area. But God, who alone could have settled the issue, remained aloof unless, as some Plymouth observers thought, the intruders' loss at sea of two "shallops going to Coonigtecutt" was to be construed as the Deity's word in the matter. To Bradford, "shuch crosses they meete with in their beginings; which some imputed as a correction from God for their intrution (to the wrong of others) into that place." And he adds his customary disclaimer: "But I dare not be bould with Gods judgments in this kind" (II, 232).

In some cases, Bradford does not even hint at a corrective purpose or at a providential origin of the calamities he records — especially those that befell Plymouth. Thus he foregoes all mention of God in connection with a hurricane which in 1635 caused extensive damage to ships and buildings. He contents himself with giving a detailed description, omitting any speculation as to divine intention behind the event. Sometimes Bradford in describing a disaster mentions God but hazards no theory as to His designs in permitting the event to occur. In his annal for 1633, he records the following: "It pleased the Lord to visite them this year with an infectious fevoure, of which many fell very sicke, and upward of ·20· persons dyed...," including several "of their anciente friends which had lived in Holand" (II, 171). But he makes no attempt to explain why the Lord might have sent this epidemic, which was so deadly to some of the holiest people in the colony, the brethren from Holland. Instead, in the next paragraph, as if to dispel any suspicion of prolonged divine displeasure, he informs the reader that "it pleased the Lord to inable them this year to send home a great quantity of beaver..." (II, 172). Yet, when he elsewhere muses on the great age to which many of the Pilgrims lived, despite their sufferings, he does not hesitate to attribute the phenomenon to God's direct concern for his faithful (II, 351).

In many other cases, as will be seen, Bradford endeavors to show how the misfortunes that the colonists suffered, such as the disruptive presence of Lyford among them, were either blessings in disguise or admonitions from God. Nor does he make any claim that all should be smooth sailing for the "saints"; his attitude about the decline of Plymouth church, already discussed, is evidence that he believed the contrary. On the other hand, he does not frequently engage in jeremiads against the settlers, blaming their troubles on their lax ways, every time some setback occurs, as the Massachusetts Bay preachers did at the outbreak of King Philip's War or on the occasion of Governor Andros's suppression of New England liberties.

VI   *God in Partnership with His Elect*

In Bradford's speculations about the longevity of many of the Pilgrims, he touches upon a type of providence quite different from the "spetial" ones that God used to save His elect in emergencies or to punish or warn the wicked or backsliding. The long-lived Pilgrims attained their advanced years obviously because they were God's "instruments" (II, 282) (a favorite phrase of Bradford's and one common in religious writing in that era) in carrying out that part of the divine plan that centered upon New England. These "instruments" were the elect, God's chosen ones; and they lived always in cheerful submission to the heavenly will. Long-range partnerships of this sort between God and man were more significant, more basic in the accomplishment of divine ends, than were sudden and unpredictable "spetiall" providences like shipwrecks, epidemics, or tempests.

Thus, in the Leyden congregation's agonizing deliberations as to whether or not the members should immigrate to the New World and expose themselves to the enormous and well-known risks of such a venture, they concluded that any difficulties they might encounter would not be insurmountable. "It might be sundrie of the things feared, might never befale; others by providente care and the use of good means, might in a great measure be prevented; and all of them (through the help of God) by fortitude, and patience, might either be borne, or overcome" (I, 60). This focus centers upon human efforts, and God has been relegated to parentheses. Nonetheless, He is still a presence, and His help, essential to the success of the undertaking, is counted on or perhaps even taken for granted by this group of the elect. For how else could it be? God would be expected to help His people, and this expectation is alluded to almost as an afterthought, so self-evident did it seem. But human virtues — patience and fortitude — and ingenuity ("good means") must also be brought to bear, if God's help is to become a reality.

The same assumption that God will help His chosen ones is expressed more succinctly in a letter written to the Virginia Company by John Robinson and William Brewster, the two men whom Bradford revered above all others. One of the arguments that the two give in their efforts to win support for their project is as follows: "We veryly beleeve and trust the Lord is with us, unto whom and whose service we have given ourselves in many trialls; and that he will graciously prosper our indeavours according to the simplicitie of our harts therin" (I, 75–76).

This assumption that the congregation is in a sort of working partnership with God in which His deputies are carrying out His plans is far more than a blind faith that God, by some "spetiall providence," will extricate them from every danger or mistake. Theirs is, rather, a long-term providence in which human beings by their devoted efforts play a major role by making their choices and by exerting their wills in conformity with what they deem to be God's desire for them. They are not, however, totally free agents, though some theologians would argue that they were. At any moment they could become either the victims or the beneficiaries of one of God's "spetiall providences"; and of course their state of grace or lack of grace, and hence their propensities to do good or evil, were entirely determined by predestination. Yet, mysteriously perhaps but nonetheless definitely, they were responsible for their own acts; for, as the Westminster Confession of faith asserts, no "violence [is] offered to the will of the creatures"[10] by God's eternal decrees.

VII   *Free Will and God's Will*

The functioning of freedom of choice and action throughout *Of Plimmoth Plantation* must be carefully examined. Bradford asserts that the migration of the Pilgrims from Holland to America was an act of "their owne free choyse and motion" (I, 45). Only after careful deliberation, doubtless interspersed with prayer, was their decision reached; and the same may be said of all the major decisions of the group: the choice of the site of Plymouth for their settlement; the sending of expeditions against the Indians; the methods adopted for dealing with troublemakers, with crime, with the weakening of religion; the various steps taken to resolve grave financial difficulties. Life at Plymouth, especially for its governor and his assistants, entailed a constant succession of critical decisions; and in no instance did God influence these decisions by direct communication from heaven, nor was such communication expected. Their guides were their own judgments and consciences. After a decision had been made and put into effect, God might vouchsafe various signs indicative of His approval; but there was no compulsion or specific individual demand from on high before the step had been taken.

Yet, in exercising their freedom of will, the Pilgrims, or at least their spiritual and temporal leaders, never forgot their ultimate dependence on God. While exploring the shores of Cape Cod after the crossing from England, the scouting party encountered gales that broke the mast of their shallop and carried away their sail. They kept up their courage, however, and after a struggle made a harbor, but only by "Gods mercie" (I, 173). Similarly, during the sickness after the arrival at Plymouth, a certain few of the colonists, remaining healthy, worked tirelessly in caring for the ill, for "the Lord ... upheld" (I, 196) them.

The difference between "spetiall providences" and the divine support supplied in these two incidents, which have been chosen at random from the many examples, is immediately apparent. Human effort counts for much in them, though, as Bradford warns elsewhere, "a mans way is not in his owne power; God can make the weake to stand; let him also that standeth take heed least he fall" (I, 297). Or, as John Robinson stated in a letter to John Carver in 1620, "The spirite of a man (sustained by the spirite of God) will sustaine his infirmitie..." (I, 129).

This seeming collaboration between God and His elect is even more impressive when it can be discerned in operation over long periods of time. Brewster and Robinson had assured the Virginia Company that God favored the Pilgrim venture; and, by the end of 1629, nine years after the voyage of the *Mayflower,* Bradford was convinced that the colony was a success — that God had indeed approved it. The signs were numerous and unmistakable. For example, in that year and the next, a number of the Leyden people had finally rejoined their brethren at Plymouth. This reunion with at least part of the old congregation could only be interpreted as a token of divine satisfaction with years of prayerful and patient effort.

In 1629 and 1630, the great migration of Puritans to Massachusetts Bay had also begun; indeed, some of the Leyden people had crossed on the ships that brought the first sizable contingents of Bay settlers — who soon were to far outnumber the Plymouth colonists. Relative to this situation, Bradford wrote that this arrival was "the beginning of a larger harvest unto the Lord, in the increase of his churches and people in these parts, to the admiration of many, and allmost wonder of the world; that of so small beginnings so great things should issue.... But it was the Lords doing, and it ought to be marvellous in our eyes" (II, 63).

Though rejoicing at the arrival of the Leyden brethren, Bradford calls attention to the monetary cost incurred by the colonists in paying the passage of many of them to Plymouth and in maintaining them until they could become self-supporting. Though Bradford gives no definite figure, one may be sure that the expenditure was a heavy burden, nor was repayment either asked or expected. In this really major sacrifice on the part of the planters, Bradford rightly discerns "a rare example ... of brotherly love, and Christian care in performing their promises and covenants to their bretheren...";and he marvels "that these poore people here in a willderness should ... be inabled in time to repay all these ingagments, and many more unjustly brought upon them through the unfaithfullness of some..." (II, 68). Bradford sees "more then of man in these acheevements," and discerns "the spetiall worke and hand of God" (II, 68). But man *was* in them.

So convinced was Bradford that God was employing human beings at Plymouth as means to His ends that he included the idea in the opening sentence of the legal document whereby in 1641 he transferred to the freemen of Plymouth the previous patent of the colony, one which he had held in his own name since its acquisition some years before. The document begins: "Whereas ... William Bradford, and diverce others the first instruments of God in the beginning of this great work of plantation..." (II, 282).

Bradford's most analytical as well as most eloquent statement about the peculiarly favorable status that the Pilgrims enjoyed with God is in that section of his *History,* already mentioned, where he discusses the longevity of the colonists. To begin with, it must be borne in mind that longevity *per se* would be of great significance to such a devoted reader of the Bible as Bradford, for the patriarchs of the Old Testament customarily attained superhuman ages. Why should not the patriarchs of New Plymouth be similarly distinguished? Delightedly, Bradford discovers that to a lesser degree they were, and he proceeds to list those qualities in their characters which caused them to be thus singled out. Certainly, he states, their physical circumstances were not conducive to robust health but were inimical to long life what with "chaing of aeir, famine, or unholsome foode, much drinking of water..." (II, 351). Also, in the Apostle's words (II Corinthians XI. 26, 27), they journeyed "often, in the perils of waters, in perills of robers, in perills of their owne nation, in perils among the heathen, in perills in the willdernes, in perills in the sea, in perills among false breethern..." (II, 352). Bradford must have been thrilled by this passage which so exactly described the experiences of the Pilgrims and which made it possible to compare them with the founders of the primitive Christian church that the Separatists were laboring under such great handicaps to restore. There is no more striking example of biblical typology in *Of Plimmoth Plantation.*

What then did account for the prolonged life spans of the many of the Pilgrims? Obviously, of course, God "upheld them" (II, 352) as "useful instrumentes"; but the quality of their lives must also have been a factor. These aged persons must have practiced the same piety, held the same faith, and exhibited the same steadfastness of purpose that characterized the patriarchs whom they so closely resembled. Bradford suggests the possibility that

God, in upholding the faithful Pilgrims, was presenting an example, a lesson, for the edification of mankind. "God, it seems, would have all men to behold and observe such mercies and works of his providence as these are towards his people, that they in like cases might be incouraged to depend upon God in their trials, and also blese his name when they see his goodnes towards others. Man lives not by bread only, Deut: 8.3" (II, 352).

Bradford had quoted the second sentence of this Deuteronomy passage earlier in *Of Plimmoth Plantation* when he described the near famine of 1623; but, in reconsidering the matter, he wonders whether the austere diets forced on the Pilgrims might not have been God's way of keeping them healthy; and he mentions Daniel and Jacob as Old Testament persons who thrived on simple or inadequate fare. Bradford saw a special value in a faith that could accept, or wait out, adversity and hardship until they eventuated in benefit to the afflicted, as they invariably must when God is dealing with His elect. But neither the biblical nor the Plymouth patriarchs were passive, for their own exertions and faith enabled God to transform their hardships into blessings.

Even the near collapse of the colony brought about by Lyford's and Oldham's machinations could turn out to be a blessing; for, after the exposure of those two conspirators and their banishment, many persons "who before stood something of from the church, now seeing Lyford's unrighteous dealing, and malignitie against the church, now tendered themselves to the church, and were joyned to the same.... And so these troubles prodused a quite contrary effecte in sundrie hear, then these adversaries hoped for. Which was looked at as a greate worke of God, to draw on men by unlickly means; and that in reason which might rather have set them further of" (I, 406–407). Yet the goal of the authorities in chastising these malefactors was necessary in the producing of these results.

To Bradford, it must be remembered, the salvation of souls by their being drawn into the church was the most glorious of all the works of God, who alone supplies the grace necessary to this end, the church serving only as a means. For the Plymouth congregation unexpectedly to find its numbers swelling with these new converts must have been gratifying indeed and cause for renewed thankfulness to God and ample recompense for the efforts of the townspeople in exposing evil. In any case, misfortunes like famine or social or political turmoil could be blessings in disguise — or, Brad-

ford states elsewhere, could be the means by which God had chosen
to deal "with his people to teach them, and humble them, that he
may doe them good in the later end" (II, 131). But the people had
to exert themselves in order to reap such benefits. Trial by existence, as Robert Frost calls it, is not a passive process; it demands
an active human participation.

It is also true that the faithful in time of trial and trouble always
had recourse to prayer with an expectation of being heard. Prayer,
Bradford avers, saved a group of the Scrooby Separatists from
shipwreck on their way from England to Holland "when mans
hope, and helpe wholy failed..." (I, 33). Again, during the disas-
trous drought of 1623, the planters "sett a parte a solemne day of
humilliation, to seeke the Lord by humble and fervente prayer, in
this great distrese. And he was pleased to give them a gracious and
speedy answer, both to their owne, and the Indeans admiration,
that lived amongest them" (I, 324–25) — the answer was the onset
of "shuch sweete and gentle showers, as gave them cause of
rejoyceing, and blessing God" (I, 325). But prayer, too, was an act
of free will, and it presupposed a sort of partnership between God
and His human instruments. The calming of a storm or the sending
of rain in a drought might resemble special providences, but they
were direct consequences of a human act of supplication. They
were neither arbitrary nor unexpected, as, for example, were the
coming of Squanto or the deflection of the arrows in the first
encounter with the Indians.

VIII   *The Place of Plymouth in God's Plan for the World*

The ultimate assumption, and one that Bradford readily made,
was that the Plymouth venture was a part — and an important part
— of God's overall plan to restore true Christianity to the world.
This belief is implicit in the very first pages of the *History,* in which
Bradford gives a brief outline of the Reformation in England from
1550 onward. In this movement, which he recognizes as involving
much of Europe, he places the activities of the Separatists in and
around the hamlet of Scrooby — activities in which he himself
played a part. When the King and the bishops were finally over-
thrown, he rejoiced from faraway Plymouth; and, in 1646, he
added to *Of Plimmoth Plantation* a paean on the triumph of the
nonconformists — "A late observation," he calls it, "as it were by
the way, worthy to be noted" (I, 14). That he placed the "observa-

tion" in the section of the book devoted to the early history of the Separatists rather than in whatever stage of the book he might have reached at the time is significant.

The Puritan Revolution was a culmination, he correctly thought, of the movements in whose beginnings he had had a role, however humble and obscure. The "observation" is composed mainly of biblical quotations appropriate to and prophetic of the event. The most exultant passage is that in which he urges his fellow colonists to recognize their contribution to the success of a divinely intended historical movement: "Doe you not now see the fruits of your labours, O all yee servants of the Lord? that have suffered for his truth, and have been faithfull witneses of the same, and yee little handfull amongst the rest, the least amongest the thousands of Israll? You have not only had a seede time, but many of you have seene the joyefull Harvest" (I, 15).

For many years Bradford had been convinced of the vital role that the Plymouth church had played in the progress of the Reformation, for he had evidence that its example caused the Massachusetts Bay settlers to adopt, in 1630, the Congregational form of church government — to him, the only biblically sanctioned polity. The Puritan Revolution in England was primarily effected and dominated at its inception by the Presbyterians, whose system of church government by a hierarchy of ruling bodies was displeasing to the Separatists. Yet Bradford and other Separatists agreed with Presbyterian theology, which was Calvinistic, and they shared the Presbyterian opposition to the Anglican episcopacy. In New England, where Presbyterianism did not thrive, Congregationalism flourished from the start. The Pilgrim church, of course, had always been Congregationalist.

Controversy continues to this day as to whether or not the Puritan immigrants to Massachusetts Bay in 1629 and 1630 were already disposed toward Congregationalism before their departure from England or whether they adopted it under the influence of the New Plymouth "saints," with whom they established almost immediate contact. One thing is certain: Deacon Samuel Fuller of Plymouth, who acted as physician for the colony, was sent to minister to the sick among the immigrants at Salem and the Bay immediately after their arrival; and, during his visit, he entered into discussions about matters of theology and church governance. Letters written on these occasions by Fuller and Governor Endecott of Salem indicate at least an agreement that the Congregational way was the one prescribed in the New Testament and suggest that perhaps Deacon Fuller had been instrumental in heading the newcomers in that direction.

This latter view seems to have been shared by Bradford, who, looking back from the 1640s, wrote in his terminal paragraph for the year 1630: "Thus out of smalle beginings greater things have been produced by his hand that made all things of nothing, and gives being to all things that are; and as one small candle may light a thousand, so the light here [doubtless Bradford means Plymouth] kindled hath shone to many, yea in some sorte to our whole nation; let the glorious name of Jehova have all the praise" (II, 117). Massachusetts Bay may have been, in Winthrop's hopeful words, "a city on a hill," but Plymouth was a candle to light thousands on their way to salvation through a church founded after the ordinances of Christ and the Apostles. Such was God's providence.

IX   *Biblical Justification*

Thus, convinced that they were serving God in the working out of His intentions, groups like the Pilgrims and the Massachusetts Bay settlers naturally searched the Bible for justification and encouragement in their undertakings. The Bible to all English Protestants was the one book by which a Christian had to interpret his own life and discover his reason for existence. All Puritan writings are replete with biblical quotations, paraphrases, and allusions; and *Of Plimmoth Plantation* is typical in this respect. In this study, many scriptural references (though only a small fraction of the total) have already been alluded to; but focus should now be directed on several biblical texts which are fundamental to Bradford's view of life and history and hence to the purpose of his book.

It has been seen that, to Bradford, his wandering band of "saints" was reliving the lives of both the ancient Israelites and the Apostles. Assuming these roles, the "saints" were seeking a promised land, attempting to return to Zion, and struggling to reestablish the primitive Christian church — and all three purposes merged into one. The Old and New Testament themes of exile, return, and struggle for purity and salvation were to Bradford the themes of his and his brethren's lives. He makes this conviction very clear in a paraphrase from Hebrews II:13–16 (already quoted, *supra*, p. 35) at the beginning of Chapter VII of the *History,* where he describes the departure from Leyden: "So they lefte the goodly and pleasante citie . . . but they knew they were pilgrimes. . ." (I, 124).

The parallels between biblical events and the trials of the Pilgrims are persistently apparent to Bradford throughout his narrative. When part of the original group of immigrants had to be left behind in England because of the unseaworthiness of the ship that was to have accompanied the *Mayflower,* Bradford finds a precedent in Deuteronomy 20:5–8: "And thus, like Gedions armie, this small number was devided, as if the Lord by this worke of his providence thought these few to many for the great worke he had to doe" (I, 138–40). When the Pilgrims found the cache of Indian corn on Cape Cod and carried some of it back to the ship, Bradford found a similarity with an episode recounted in Numbers 13:23–26: The returning party, "like the men from Eshcoll carried with them of the fruits of the land, and showed their breethren. . ." (I, 165). (Perhaps the biblical parallel assuaged Bradford's conscience for his theft of the Indians' food.)

In fact, the whole history of the nonconformists before the overthrow of the king and bishops was to Bradford reminiscent of the captivity and exile of the Jews; and, at the time of the Puritan revolution, he quoted Psalm 126 in the Geneva translation with what seemed to him complete appropriateness. The Pilgrims now "may say (among the thousands of Israll) when the Lord brougt again the captivite of Zion, we were like them that dreame . . . The lord hath done greate things for us, wherof we rejoyce . . . They that sowe in teares, shall reap in joye. They wente weeping, and carried precious seede, but they shall returne with joye, and bring their sheaves" (I, 15).

Indeed, Bradford was so convinced that Plymouth colony played an integral, if small, part in God's strategy for the reformation of His church that all statements — some by well-known scholars[11] — that Bradford had given up all hope for Plymouth by the time he ceased writing *Of Plimmoth Plantation* are to be subjected to profound skepticism. The verses from Psalm 126 quoted in the preceding paragraph were added to the history in 1646, the year of his final annal. The quotation and the whole passage in which it is contained are expressions of jubilation as well as of self-congratulation for the little colony that had performed so well its divinely assigned duties.

CHAPTER 6

Minor Prose and Linguistic Interests

T HOUGH *Of Plimmoth Plantation* is the work upon which William Bradford's literary reputation must rest, a number of other writings from his pen are extant. Among them are a section of the promotional tract, *Mourt's Relation,* published in London in 1622 to encourage immigration to New England; a sizable number of letters, most of them in Bradford's so-called *Letter Book,* which he compiled and edited; two theological tracts, or *Dialogues;* and a small body of verse. The *Dialogues* and the poems, both of which are for the most part the work of Bradford's years after he terminated his *History* about 1647, show him to have been deeply preoccupied not only with theology but with the study of the ancient languages that he deemed essential for successful study of the Bible and church history. These linguistic interests demand some attention if one is to understand fully the richness of Bradford's character and talents.

I   Mourt's Relation

In November 1621, when the ship *Fortune* arrived in Plymouth Harbor carrying thirty-nine new settlers, Deacon Robert Cushman, who had been a member of the Leyden church since 1609, was on board; for he had come as liaison man for the London adventurers. After a stay of about a month, he departed on the *Fortune* for the return voyage to England, and he carried with him material for the book that was later to be known as *Mourt's Relation* (1622). The book is important in that it provides many details otherwise unrecorded concerning the first year of the English at Plymouth, and it is also of great interest because some of it that was written by William Bradford became the only substantial portion of his writing that was published in his lifetime.

Mourt's Relation is, however, in every way a less important and impressive work than *Of Plimmoth Plantation*. Its purpose was entirely different, for it belonged to that body of colonial American writing classified by literary historians as promotional tracts. Selected phrases from its title, which fills a whole page, sufficiently indicate its nature: "A Relation or Journall of the beginning and Proceedings of the English plantation settled at Plimoth . . . with [the Settlers'] difficult passage, their safe arrivall, their joyfull building of, and comfortable planting themselves in the now well defended Towne. . . . "[1] Sections of the book itself, as one commentator has said, read like sales talk for Florida real estate.[2]

The book is the work of several hands. Cushman contributed the opening dedication "To His Much respected Friend, Mr. I.P." (that is, John Pierce, the recipient of the first Plymouth patent), who is respectfully begged to accept as wholly truthful "this poore Relation . . . as being writ by the severall Actors themselves, after their plaine and rude manner. . . . "[3] There follows an address "To the Reader," signed by G. Mourt, in which assurance is given that, with God's help, the infant colony, despite some early setbacks, is on its way to achieving its two chief ends — that of spreading the Gospel and that of procuring "unto themselves and others a quiet and comfortable habitation."

Mourt also makes clear that he is the editor or compiler of the volume; he is using material that came to his hand from his "both known and faithful friends, on whose writings"[4] he heavily relies. Following this effusion is reprinted John Robinson's letter (which is also in *Of Plimmoth Plantation*) to the Pilgrims as they were about to sail for Southampton. Finally the *Relation* itself is given in five episodes, and the book ends with statements and arguments, one by Robert Cushman, that offer inducements to prospective colonists. It is fair to say that the real and deplorable state of affairs at Plymouth was not misrepresented but was simply ignored.

The identity of Mourt has never been definitely established, but strong evidence points to his being George Morton, a member of the Leyden church who was active in the negotiations leading to the colonizing venture, who later went to Plymouth, who died soon after his arrival, and whose son Nathaniel wrote *New Englands Memoriall* (1669). If George Morton actually prepared the *Relation,* the question remains as to why he did not sign his real name to the Preface. The most likely answer is that a typographical error was perpetrated or that Morton, considering the antagonism in official circles against Separatists, did not wish to publicize his connection with the Pilgrims' activities.

There is general agreement that the narrative portions of *Mourt's Relation* were written by Edward Winslow and William Bradford — that is, they were copied, perhaps with considerable editing, from journals kept by them and carried to England by Deacon Cushman. There is, however, less general agreement as to which man wrote the different parts of the narrative, but the surmises made by Henry Marlyn Dexter in his scholarly edition of the *Relation* (1865) are as acceptable as any and will be the basis for discussion here. The book actually consists of five separate "relations," and each is about a different period or episode in the first year of the colony's history. The first and by far the longest of these narrations — attributed to Bradford — covers the landing at Cape Cod, the exploration, the establishment of the settlement at Plymouth, and the first encounters and transactions with the Indians.

Among the several reasons for assigning this lengthy section to Bradford is the similarity of some of its phrasing with that in *Of Plimmoth Plantation* about the same events. Another is the fact that Edward Winslow seems not to have been a member of one or perhaps two of the scouting sorties that were described in detail. On the other hand, it appears more than probable that Winslow composed the accounts embodied in the four other "relations," all rather short, which describe a visit to Massasoit; an expedition to recover a boy lost among the Nauset Indians; an expedition to rescue Squanto, supposedly held by the hostile Corbitant; and, finally, a fur-trading trip to Massachusetts Bay.

Assuming that the long first narrative is from Bradford's pen — and most certainly it is at least partly so — one may make some interesting comparisons of its style and its general approach to its material with those of the *History.* To begin with, there is much less moralizing, philosophizing, and theologizing in *Mourt's Relation.* References to providence are less numerous, though there is a sprinkling of them, to assure the reader — who might be thinking of immigration — that God favored the colony. In general, the tone and style are chatty and matter-of-fact, for the obvious intent is to convey information in the same informal manner as in a conversation in which one practical person provides factual details to another equally practical. The account is much fuller than that for the similar period and events in *Of Plimmoth Plantation,* and in the latter work Bradford, referring apparently to *Mourt's Relation,* directs the reader seeking more details to "a Jurnall made by one of the company; and some other passages of jurneys and relations allredy published. . ." (I, 212–13).[5]

To this day *Mourt's Relation* remains fascinating reading but for reasons different from those which would have made it appealing in the seventeenth century. In the first place, for the modern reader it is the earliest of many works that provide extensive information concerning the geography, the human inhabitants, the resources, and the climate of Cape Cod. As such a source, *Mourt's Relation* deserves shelf space beside such books as H. D. Thoreau's *Cape Cod* (1865) and Henry Beston's *The Outermost House* (1928). As for the "plaine and rude manner"[6] in which Cushman says *Mourt's Relation* is written, most readers will agree that the style is plain, especially when compared to the ornate prose of many writers of the period, but the adjective *rude* is not applicable. Simplicity, directness, concreteness, a noticeable lack of allusion, whether classical or biblical, do not constitute rudeness but contribute instead to effectiveness in narrative and descriptive writing — at least by present-day standards. The merits of the book as a whole, both in style and content, were indeed soon recognized; for in 1624 Captain John Smith included an abstract of it in his *General Historie of Virginia, New England, and the Summer Isles,* and the 1625 edition of *Purchas His Pilgrims* contains a condensation of it.

II *First* Dialogue

During the last ten years of his life, William Bradford, concerned as he was about the decline in religious zeal in his community, devoted considerable time and effort to an assessment of his and his people's spiritual experiences from the beginnings of the church at Scrooby to the establishment of the Congregational way of worship on a firm footing in New England. The result was three dialogues or conferences — of which the first and the third are extant — between the young and the "ancient" men of the colony; and these conversations are clearly designed to inform the rising generation about the nature of their religion and about the cost at which freedom to follow it had been achieved. Bradford apparently hoped that knowledge of their religious heritage and of its martyrs would inspire the young people to greater piety and to a stronger sense of spiritual community. To a considerable extent, *Of Plimmoth Plantation* had been written with this same purpose; but it was not solely exhortatory and included much more than theological discussion or chuch history. The *Dialogues*, at least the two still in existence, were entirely devoted to ecclesiastical and theological matters.

The first of these pieces was rather ponderously titled *A Dialogue or the sume of a Conference between som younge men borne in New England and sundery Ancient men that came out of holland and old England,* and it is dated "Anno dom 1648."[7] Several pages of this work exist in Bradford's own hand, but the complete text has survived only in the *Plymouth Church Records,* into which it was copied by Bradford's nephew, Nathaniel Morton, the clerk of both the town and colony of Plymouth — presumably in 1680, the same year in which he transcribed large portions of his uncle's history into the *Church Records.* The first printed appearance was in Alexander Young's *Chronicles of the Pilgrim Fathers* (1841). The Colonial Society of Massachusetts reproduced it much later with the original punctuation and spelling in Volume XXII (1920) of its *Publications.*

This first *Dialogue* is not a literary triumph. Its style is cramped and unclear; and the dialogue form, very popular at the time Bradford wrote, can be described only as a clumsy contrivance. Very likely Bradford participated in many religious discussions involving the young and the old, for theology was a major topic of conversation in New England until well into the nineteenth century; but it is highly unlikely that any such conferences took the form in which Bradford presents them. In both the first and third *Dialogues,* the young men do all the listening — as they were probably expected to do — while the ancient men expound history and theology. Most unlikely of all, however, is the ease with which the young are convinced of the correctness of their elders' opinions. Nonetheless, these dialogues are valuable and interesting, first, as records of the firsthand experiences of persons who had been involved in the religious upheavals of Renaissance England and, second, as statements of Separatist doctrines.

A principal purpose of the first *Dialogue* was to play down differences among the Separatists, the Presbyterians, and the other nonconforming churches. Bradford makes very clear, as had Separatists for the past two or three generations, that his sect did not like a "Nicke Name" like "Brownists" or "Puritant" (117) to be applied to them. The name Brownist was particularly obnoxious to them, partly because Robert Browne himself had renounced the Separatist principles that he had once promulgated and had rejoined the national church, but mainly because the name tended to obscure the fact that the Separatists were followers of Christ after the fashion of the pure, primitive church and were not the disciples of any one latter-day reformer. Bradford's point, which he approaches from several directions, is the Augustinian and Calvinist one that there is "a Catholique Church or ... misticall body of Christ" composed of God's elect "or visible Christians ... dispersed upon the face of the whole earth" (116). The New England congregations are a part of this body of Christ, but members of other churches are represented in it as well. Among its numbers, indeed, were many individuals and some entire congregations that worshiped after the basically unsound manner of the Church of England.

Bradford naturally extols the Congregational way, in which the elect enter into a church covenant and duly choose their pastors, teachers, elders, and deacons. He decries promiscuous acceptance of the unregenerate, along with the regenerate persons, to full membership and communion; he takes a dim view of the Presbyterian system of governance; and he deplores the imposition of clergy upon a congregation by prelates or other authorities. Yet, following John Robinson's lead, he agrees quite readily that churches in which any or all of these questionable practices obtain may contain on the spiritual level numbers of regenerate believers tacitly or implicitly covenanted with a minister completely acceptable to them. In other words, literal adherence to Congregational doctrine and polity, including written covenants, was not absolutely necessary, but was highly desirable.

This conciliatory attitude stands in marked contrast to the doctrinaire rigidity commonly associated with the religious controversies that raged during the English Reformation. Bradford was himself a conciliator, but even John Robinson had retreated somewhat from his first uncompromising Separatist views, which with considerable justification were called Brownist. Thus Bradford, taking his cue from Robinson, rather deplores the "Ridgednes of Separation" (117), and he seems to have gone a long way toward the viewpoint of the churches of Massachusetts Bay, which were Congregational and nonconformist but not Separatist. Moreover, Bradford cites John Cotton's rejection of the word Separatism in his *The Way of the Congregational Churches Cleared* (1648) that was written in the same year as the first *Dialogue* and that was much admired by Bradford.

Another matter that Bradford touches upon in the first *Dialogue* is "the exercise of Prophesye that is that men out of office haveing Gifts may upon occasion edify the Church publickly and oppenly and applying the Scriptures which seemes to be a New practice" (118). The reference is to the custom, at the time, in the Congregational churches of permitting members of the laity to participate actively in preaching the word — a practice suggestive of that followed in Quaker meetings. This sort of prophesying seems to have been the rule at Plymouth, and it must have been relied upon heavily during the years when the church there had no ordained pastor or teacher. An interesting glimpse of a Plymouth church meeting is given by Governor Winthrop, who visited there in October 1632, when Roger Williams was serving as teacher and Ralph Smith as pastor: "On the Lord's Day was a sacrament, which they did partake in; and in the afternoon Mr. Roger Williams (according to their custom) propounded a question, to which Mr. Smith, spake briefly; then Mr. Williams prohesied; and after the Governor of Plimouth [Bradford] spake to the question; after him the elder [Brewster]; then some two or three more of the congregation."[8]

Bradford defends prophesying on Scriptural grounds by asserting that it was practiced in the primitive church and by quoting John Cotton and John Robinson in its support. Bradford, however, agrees with these clerical authorities that only a few specially gifted laymen in each congregation are capable of prophecy. It is significant that a hundred years later the Reverend Thomas Prince of Boston included in his *Chronological History of New England* the passage from Winthrop just quoted. In addition to changing the tense to the present, Prince inserted in brackets the information that Bradford was a student of Hebrew and that Brewster was a learned man.[9] In other words, not every one was expected to prophesy — a situation that would lessen the prestige of the clergy. That Bradford was among the eligible ones is a testimony to the esteem in which his attainments were held.

In addition to discussions of theology and ecclesiastical polity, Bradford's first *Dialogue* includes much biographical information concerning the earliest Separatists in England and contains brief sketches of a number of them, including Henry Ainsworth, John Robinson, and Richard Clyfton. Bradford without doubt intended that these worthies should serve as models of piety and selflessness for the young men to emulate. One consequence was that he touched only very lightly upon the ruinous dissensions among the English Separatists in Amsterdam and scarcely alluded to the scandalous sexual excesses of one of that church's elders.[10] In fact, the reason the Pilgrims removed to Leyden after a year was to escape the outrageous state of affairs among the Amsterdam Separatists. Where silence would best serve his purpose, Bradford was silent.

III   *Third* Dialogue

In 1652, Bradford composed *A Dialogue or · 3ᵈ· Conference betweene some Yonge-men borne in New-England, and some Ancient-men, which came out of Holand and Old England, concerning the Church, and the govermente therof.*[11] By this time, he had ceased all writing in *Of Plimmoth Plantation,* including the genealogical entries at the end. At any rate, since writing the first *Dialogue* in 1648, Bradford had been concentrating more and more on the life of the mind and of the spirit. On two pages in the front of the manuscript booklet (in Bradford's hand) that contains the third *Dialogue* are written the Hebrew and Greek alphabets with the names of the letters in Roman characters. Eight pages following the *Dialogue* itself are devoted to quotations in Hebrew from the Old Testament with accompanying English translations from the Geneva Bible. Furthermore, on the cover page of the manuscript containing the third *Dialogue* is a Hebrew verse (Proverbs 21:30), and on the title page of the *Dialogue* proper are three brief passages in Hebrew from the Psalms (26:8; 16:5; and 26:5).[12] The *Dialogue* ends with the last verse, in Greek, of the Epistle to the Romans, the English rendering of which is: "To God only wise, be glory through Jesus Christ forever. Amen." Throughout the body of the work are found sprinklings of Hebrew and Greek and some rather liberal infusions of Latin — flourishes which are not to be found in the first *Dialogue.*

As will be seen later, Bradford's involvement with ancient languages, especially Hebrew, is an interesting and significant aspect of his life and character. By the time he wrote the third *Dialogue,* he was able to use his linguistic learning with some ease and grace; and he perhaps achieved thereby the goal of impressing the less learned young men whose religious consciousness the "ancient men" were attempting to sharpen. At any rate, whatever the impact and the function of the linguistic embellishments, the third

Dialogue is a forceful piece of polemical writing that is far superior
to the first in organization, clarity, and liveliness of style. Its main
purpose is to describe and discuss four forms of Church government — the "Papist," the Episcopal (Church of England), the
Presbyterian, and the Independent or Congregational — with the
intent of demonstrating to the young men that the Congregational
way is the closest to primitive Christian practice and hence the most
pleasing to God.

The *Dialogue's* opening and longest and most spirited section
deals with Roman Catholicism. As an outburst of prejudice, it
holds its own in scurrility among the numerous anti-Catholic dia-
tribes of the Reformation. There is no need to recapitulate Bradford's attacks on Rome; none are original, and all have been extant
for the past four hundred years. Bradford's major thesis is the
same as that of most Reformation polemicists: "Extra bibliam non
est veritas infallibilis"[13] — except for the Bible, there is no infalli-
ble truth. The Popes, Bradford asserts in chorus with thousands of
other reformers, have substituted themselves in the place of the
Bible and have thus earned themselves such titles, to mention but a
few, as anti-Christ, man of sin, whore of Babylon.

As Bradford warms to his subject, he quotes or cites a battalion
of anti-Roman writers as he launches into an area that might well
have piqued the interest of the young men, arousing them from the
very probable soporific influence of the "ancient men's" previous
discourses. For six pages Bradford goes into detail concerning the
alleged sodomy, incest, fornication, adultery, "and other vitiouse
practices" (421) that he would have his listeners believe were
indulged in as a matter of course by Popes, bishops, and cardinals.
Indeed, one cannot refrain from suspecting that Bradford himself
might have experienced a certain pleasure in reciting at such length
and in such detail these multitudinous abominations. Involved, of
course, is considerable self-righteousness for, to Bradford, nothing
the Roman Church did or stood for was acceptable. He is critical
even of Roman reliance on the Latin Vulgate Bible — an objection
which he seems to make from the vantage point of his own study of
the Hebrew and the Greek Testaments.

What follows in the *Dialogue* is relatively tame. In the discussion
of the Church of England, the "ancient men" deplore the retention
of the bishops in the national church; for they are a residue of
Rome, as is the use of vestments, certain rites, and the Book of
Common Prayer. As for basic doctrines, the Anglican Church is

not so far out of line with general Protestantism. Presbyterianism, on Bradford's diminishing scale of vituperation, fares much better. Only its superstructure of classes (the plural of *classis,* a regional organization of churches; a presbytery); its synods, which supersede individual churches in authority; the Presbyterian policy of admitting all but the most scandalous persons to church membership and to the Lord's Supper caused Bradford grave concern. But perhaps because the Presbyterians, though challenged by the Independents, wielded great power at this time in England, he judiciously refrained from severe censure.

Expectedly, the final section about Congregationalism is totally approving; for this form of church government, Bradford insists and repeats, comes closest to that directed by the New Testament. Herein lies the brightest hope for the Christian church in Plymouth and in the world. He ends by exhorting the young men to "stand fast in the libertie ... wher with Christ hath made us free. Yee have been caled unto liberty; only use not liberty for an occassion to the flesh, but by love serve one another [Galatians 5:1, 13]" (463).

IV *Letters*

Included in *Of Plimmoth Plantation* are many letters written by various persons connected with the colonization of New Plymouth or having dealings with the plantation, for Bradford seems to agree with those "wise men" who considered "letters ... the best parte of histories" (I, 106), perhaps because they constitute tangible material and not hearsay or second-hand reports. (The Puritan was a literalist both in the interpretation of the Bible and in the presentation of history.) Some of these letters are written by Bradford; some bear his signature as one of two or more senders; some are by dignitaries such as the Reverend John Robinson or Governor John Winthrop of Massachusetts Bay. Many of the letters, of course, are on rather dry business matters; others deal with more lively subjects; but almost all reveal a care and a conscious concern for style and a tendency to moralize or philosophize.

Bradford compiled a so-called *Letter Book,* which contained copies of letters written or received by him and by others in the plantation; and this work constituted a store of information that he later borrowed on heavily in writing his *History.* Indeed, this compilation of letters is in itself not only evidence that Bradford intended eventually to produce a publishable work but might have been the "scribbled writings" to which he refers in *Of Plimmoth Plantation* (I, 14). Significantly, Bradford himself, in a comment inserted between two letters, promises to "handle" certain matters "more particularly, in another treatise more at large, as I desire and purpose (if God permit) with many other things, in a better order."[14] It would seem that Bradford had thoughts, therefore, of publishing the *Letter Book* itself (though later he might have termed it "scribled") as well as a "treatise" (*Of Plimmoth Plantation*); otherwise such remarks would have been pointless.

Unfortunately the *Letter Book* exists only as a fragment. The original manuscript, along with that of Bradford's *History,* had been shelved in the years before the Revolution in Thomas Prince's library in the Old South Church in Boston, and it had disappeared, as had the *History,* in 1776 with the retreating British troops. Some years later a portion of it turned up in a grocer's shop in Halifax, whither the British had gone on abandoning Boston; but the first 339 pages were missing. The fragment that remained, itself now lost, is contained within only fifty pages of the third volume of the First Series of the *Collections of the Massachusetts Historical Society,* in which the letters were published, with modernized spelling and punctuation, in 1794. With the exception of one letter from John Robinson written in 1621, all the material in these surviving pages is dated between 1624 and 1630. It is easy to imagine the importance of much of what was contained in the missing pages.

Still, thanks to Dr. Jeremy Belknap, the historian who edited the letters, enough of the *Letter Book* is available to afford an accurate idea as to how Bradford employed its contents in writing *Of Plimmoth Plantation.* The striking thing as one compares the *Letter Book* and the *History* is the care with which Bradford abridged, paraphrased, or redistributed his raw material and was also selective and conscious of form in his *Of Plimmoth Plantation.* Some letters were omitted altogether, though they might have been summarized in a sentence or even a paragraph. Others were reproduced in part, and in one case a letter was broken into three parts, each of which was included in the *History* at an appropriate place.[15] Similarly, Bradford's rather extensive comments and explanations of the letters in his *Letter Book* appear in abridged form or are paraphrased in *Of Plimmoth Plantation,* for they are seldom verbatim. Apparently Bradford was rewriting what he had previously written, and the version in *Of Plimmoth Plantation* is usually an improvement either in conciseness or in phrasing.

An example of his method of tightening and condensing material in the *Letter Book* is afforded by his treatment of a letter written to him from London on December 22, 1624, by Robert Cushman, one of the most active promoters of Plymouth colony. The letter, quoted in full in the *Letter Book,* speaks of the critical illness of James Sherley, one of the merchant adventurers, and states Cushman's hope of returning by "the next ships." But, as it turned out, Cushman himself soon fell sick and died and Sherley recovered. In the *Letter Book,* Bradford's comment is fulsome and moralistic:

And now we lost the help of a wise and faithful friend: he wrote of the sickness and probability of the death of another; but knew not that his own was so near; what cause have we therefore ever to be ready! He purposed to be with us the next ships, but the Lord did otherwise dispose; and had appointed him a greater journey, to a better place. He was now taken from these troubles into which . . . we were so deeply plunged. And here I must leave him to rest with the Lord. And will proceed to other letters. . . . [16]

In *Of Plimmoth Plantation,* in which Bradford summarizes Cushman's letter in two sentences, one mentions the sickness of Sherley; the other states Cushman's "purpose this year to come over, and spend his days with" (I, 444) the colonists. His moralizing in the *Letter Book* is replaced by a terse comment: "But he that thus write [sic] of anothers sickness, knew not that his owne death was so near. It shows allso that a mans ways are not in his owne power, but in his hands, who hath the issues of life and death. Man m[a]y purpose, but God doth dispose" (I, 444). The brevity and objectivity of this treatment of the event seem to indicate a conscious effort on Bradford's part to fit his material to his purpose, which was not primarily to present a sermon on the uncertainty of the human lot, though some edifying remarks to that effect would seem appropriate and desirable to the Puritan mind. It was important historically to report Cushman's death, and in passing a lesson could be drawn from it.

Additional letters of William Bradford have been discovered and printed in various periodicals. Some of these are of limited interest, but others deserve more than cursory notice — among them a series of four written to John Winthrop between 1638 and 1644. [17] Chatty and friendly in tone, they reveal the warmth of their writer's personality and testify to the sincerity of the relationship between the two leaders. The contents of the letters range from such matters of gossip as the report of a monster to which Mrs. Anne Hutchinson supposedly gave birth after her banishment from Massachusetts Bay to such affairs of state as the boundary dispute between the two colonies and the threats of Indian warfare.

Another letter of great interest is the long one, already referred to, in Bradford's hand and signed by him and Isaac Allerton, which was discovered in the Public Records Office in London. Dated September 8, 1623, it constitutes a general report to the London partners about recent progress, about the present needs of the colony, and about the business matters, such as the trade with the Indians and the shipment to England of clapboards and furs, to which much space is devoted. One detects Bradford's yeoman background in the letter's plea that cattle be sent to the colonists, especially goats, which are praised as particularly useful as well as being suited to the rigorous conditions of New England. The writers of the letter, as has been seen, also go to great pains to describe and justify the attack on the Indians who had threatened Thomas Weston's settlement at Wessagusset, and they express their hope soon to be reunited in New England with the Leyden Separatists. Yet, though heavy with weighty matters, the Bradford-Allerton letter closes with a touch of humor that must have originated with Bradford, so typical is it of him. At the end of a paragraph dealing with the troublemaking "pertickulars" is the laconic comment: "...as they were welcome when they came, [so sh]all they be when they goe...."[18]

V   *"That Most Ancient Language and Holy Tongue"*

Cotton Mather in his *Magnalia Christi Americana* has referred to Bradford's learning in theology, history, and philosophy and to his mastery of Greek and Latin, adding, "but the Hebrew he most of all studied."[19] Never having attended a university, Bradford must have been self-taught, most probably with the help of William Brewster, whose extensive library — four hundred volumes at his death — was doubtless at Bradford's disposal. Included in the library were a Hebrew grammar and a Hebrew lexicon, along with other books helpful to the student of Hebrew,[20] a language which Brewster had presumably studied during his attendance at Cambridge University. However, Bradford may have begun his study of Hebrew after Brewster's death, for it was an interest of his old age, as he himself testified in a statement on the third of the eight pages of Hebrew quotations and words that precede the text in the manuscript of the *History*. The statement is in the shape of an inverted triangle representing either the Trinity or the upper portion of an hourglass — a common symbol of mortality in the seventeenth century. The words, written very likely in 1650, are as follows:

> Though I am growne aged, yet I have had a longing
> desire, to see with my owne eyes, somthing of that most
> ancient language, and holy tongue, in which the Law,
> and oracles of God were write; and in which God,
> and angels, spake to the holy patriarks of old
> time; and what names were given to things,
> from the creation. And though I cañot
> attaine to much herein, yet I am refresh-
> ed, to have seen some glimpse hereof;
> (as Moyses saw the Land of ca-
> can a farr of) my aime and
> desire is, to see how the words
> and phrases lye in the
> holy texte; and to
> discerne somewhat
> of the same,
> for my owne
> contente.[21]

Despite his enthusiasm, however, Bradford's knowledge of Hebrew was in actuality quite limited, as has been pointed out by Isidore S. Meyer.[22]

Bradford also had some familiarity with Greek, quotations in which may be found here and there in his writings (but not in *Of Plimmoth Plantation*). He evidenced, however, a much greater facility with Latin, in which he quotes with considerable frequency. His linguistic learning became most apparent in his later writings, such as the *Dialogues* and the manuscript versions of some of his poems. Thus the title page of the third *Dialogue* contains three Hebrew excerpts from the Psalms: Psalm 26:8, "Lord, I have loved the habitation of thy house, and the place where thine honor dwelleth"; the first three Hebrew words of Psalm 16:5, "The Lord is the portion of mine inheritance and of my cup..."; and the first half of Psalm 26:5, "I have hated the congregation of evil doers" (the English is that of the King James translation). The Hebrew and Latin quotations at the head of the poem "Some Observations..." are treated in Chapter 7.

CHAPTER 7

Poetry

I   *"A Little Booke with a Blacke Cover"*

O N 9/19 June 1657, William Bradford "being weake in body but in prfect [*sic*] memory haveing Defered the forming of his Will in hopes of haveing the healp of Mr. Thomas Prence therin; feeling himself ... drawing on to the conclusion of his mortall life[,] spake as followeth...."[1] — A dying man who proceeded to give instructions concerning the disposition of his estate, his listeners were Elder Thomas Cushman (Bradford's adopted son), Thomas Southworth, and Nathaniel Morton. At the end of Bradford's statement was the following: "I comend unto youer Wisdome and Descretions some smale bookes written by my owne hand to bee Improved as you shall see meet; In speciall I comend to you a little booke with a blacke cover wherin there is a word to Plymouth a word to Boston and a word to New England with sundry usefull verses[.]"[2] At nine o'clock on the evening of the same day, Bradford died at peace with himself and with his God as befitted one of the elect.

Among the small books, perhaps, was that containing *Of Plimmoth Plantation;* and perhaps another contained one or more of his *Dialogues.* The contents of the "little booke with a blacke cover," however, are the concern of this chapter. All or most of the original book has been lost, but another booklet in the library of the Massachusetts Historical Society contains the three poems that Bradford named in his will. This booklet is not in Bradford's hand but in that of John Willett, the fifteen-year-old son of Thomas Willett, one of the executors of Bradford's will and later the first English mayor of New York. In two places in the manuscript John Willett has signed his name and gives the date, in both cases 1657, the year of Bradford's death. The contents consist of six poems in the following order: (1) an untitled piece of 1168 lines, the first page of which is missing, about religious sects that were heretical from the Puritan point of view and about the need for the Presbyterians and Congregationalists to work together; (2) "A Word to New Plymouth"; (3) "A Word to New England"; (4) "Of Boston in New England"; (5) "Epitaphium Meum"; and (6) "Some Observations of God's merciful dealing with us in this wilderness, and his gracious protection over us these many years. Blessed be his name."[3]

As George Willison has stated, Bradford's heirs and executors "wisely . . . did nothing with"[4] the verses by which the governor apparently set so much store. As poetry they have nothing to commend them, even after allowance is made for young John Willett's sloppiness and carelessness in copying them — for what purpose is not known, though it has been suggested that he was simply engaged "in an educational exercise"[5] designed to improve his mind. By comparing the lengthy portion of "Some observations . . ." that exists in Bradford's hand with Willett's copy of it, the reader can readily see that Willett's frequent failures to provide a faithful rendering of the original have destroyed no work of beauty, for beauty is notably absent from Bradford's verse. Willett has managed to convey Bradford's meanings, and the meanings are all that could possibly concern the modern reader and probably all that really interested the author. The crudities of the originals have not been aggravated by the copyist's errors.

II *Puritan Poetics*

It is all too easy to belittle Bradford's poetic achievements, as will be amply evident upon a closer look at them. Yet they do deserve to be examined in the light of the generally held views among Puritans (whose aesthetic theories, of course, were held by the Separatists) about the function of poetry, for these views were not such as to stimulate composition of the highest order. It is true that the Puritans John Milton and Andrew Marvell in England, and Edward Taylor and perhaps even Anne Bradstreet in Massachusetts, produced poetry of merit, but the general run of Puritan verse, especially in New England, was rather sorry stuff. The basic Puritan position regarding all literature was that it should serve a purpose — that it should teach, inform, and perhaps exhort, and that it should perform these functions preferably in the service of religion. In his will, Bradford made evident his own orthodox Puritan motives for having written poetry, which he referred to as his "sundry usefull verses." As Perry Miller observes in his *The New England Mind: The Seventeenth Century,* "poetry existed primarily for its utility, it was foredoomed to didacticism, and because it was the most highly ornate of the arts, it was always in grave danger of overstepping proper limits and becoming pleasing for its own sake."[6]

Bradford's verse incurred no such danger, but Edward Taylor's did and, possibly for this reason, Taylor prudently refrained from publication during his lifetime and forbade it after his death. Nevertheless, the Puritans agreed that poetry could be of service in appealing to the religious feelings of persons untouched by prose. In the words of John Herbert, of whose verse the Puritans approved even if he were an Anglican, "A Verse may find him who a Sermon flies," — a remark quoted by Jonathan Mitchell in his Preface to Michael Wigglesworth's *The Day of Doom,*[7] which is a supreme realization of the Puritan theory of poetry and, incidentally, one of the most popular, as well as one of the aesthetically and morally most revolting, poems ever written in America.

The efforts of a man like Wigglesworth, who very likely could have written better poetry than *The Day of Doom,* were not to titillate the aesthetic sensitivities of a few cognoscenti but, in Kenneth Murdock's words, "to be of service to the rank and file of his readers."[8] *The Day of Doom* presumably accomplished this objective by performing the two greatest services of which the Puritan mind could conceive — those of alerting sinners to the dangers of damnation and of encouraging the elect on their journey to salvation. Along with the Bible, this poem could be found in almost every New England household for a century and a half after it was written. Wigglesworth wrote "Truths dressed up in *Plain Meeter,*"[9] as Cotton Mather said; and, like the plain style in prose, the plain meter in poetry was indispensable, a fact which accounts for the mutilation of the Psalms of David as rendered in the *Bay Psalm Book,* the authors of which piously averred that they had "attended Conscience rather than Elegance, fidelity rather than poetry.... Gods Altar" did not need their "pollishings."[10]

III   *Influence of "Englished" Psalms*

Within the context of the Puritan attitude toward poetry and its actual practice in New England by all poets except Edward Taylor and Anne Bradstreet in some of her poems, the appallingly un-poetic quality of Bradford's verse becomes understandable if not acceptable. The fact is that it was no worse and no better than that of Michael Wigglesworth or that of the authors of *The Bay Psalm Book*. It would be interesting, however, to know what models Bradford had before him when he switched in his sixtieth year from the writing of vigorous and sometimes lyric prose to the composing of deplorably bad verse. However, one need not search far to find a possible model, for one book of metered and rhymed English existed to which Bradford had been exposed continuously since its publication in 1612 and which, by its very nature, he would have inordinately admired — Henry Ainsworth's *The Book of Psalmes: Englished Both in Prose and Metre.*

Ainsworth, who was the pastor of one of the two antagonistic English Separatist churches in Amsterdam, was an able polemicist and learned scholar who was especially noted for his mastery of Hebrew. Thus when he "Englished" a psalmody, readers of literary taste would have been distressed and surprised at the crudity of the translation if religious zeal had not deadened their sensitivities. The Separatists, of course, immediately adopted Ainsworth's version for singing in their churches, and the Pilgrim congregation con-tinued to use it until 1692 when it was supplanted by the equally unliterary *Bay Psalm Book.*

What the Ainsworth psalmody meant to the Plymouth church-goers is conveyed by Longfellow in *The Courtship of Miles Standish.* John Alden, approaching Priscilla's house on his matri-monial errand, hears her voice

> Singing the hundreth Psalm, the grand old Puritan Anthem,
> Music that Luther sang to the sacred words of the Psalmist,
> Full of the breath of the Lord, consoling and comforting many.
> Then, as he opened the door, he beheld the form of the maiden
> Seated beside her wheel. . . .
> Open wide on her lap lay the well-worn psalm-book of Ainsworth,
> Printed in Amsterdam, the words and the music together,
> Rough-hewn, angular notes [the old form of musical notation],
>   like stones in the wall of a churchyard,
> Darkened and overhung by the running vine of the verses.
> Such was the book from whose pages she sang the old Puritan
>   anthem. . . . [11]

The scene, though somewhat sentimentalized, is rather appealing, but the words that Priscilla was singing, Ainsworth's rendition of the Hundredth Psalm, are disillusioning and, if Longfellow had made the mistake of including them, would have destroyed the atmosphere he was at such pains to create. Ainsworth's translation of Psalm 100 follows:

1. Shout to Jehovah, all the earth.
2. Serve ye Jehovah with gladnes: before him come with singing-merth.
3. Know that Jehovah he God is: *Its* he that made us, and not wee; his folk, and sheep of his feeding.
4. O with confession enter yee his gates, his courtyards with praising: Confess to him, bless ye his name.
5. Because Jehovah *he* good is; his mercy *is the same:* and his faith, unto all ages.[12]

With effort one can detect in this grotesque rendition semblances of meter and rhyme, but most regrettable is the distortion of natural, idiomatic English word order — "he God is," "he good is" — in the effort to achieve these semblances. What has been lost can be gauged by a comparison with the version of the same psalm in the King James Bible, one admittedly not written under the sole compulsion of producing meter and rhyme:

Make a joyful noise unto the Lord, all ye lands.
Serve the Lord with gladness: come before his presence with singing.
Know ye that the Lord he is God: it is he that hath made us, and not we ourselves; we are his people, and the sheep of his pasture.
Enter into his gates with thanksgiving, and into his courts with praise; be thankful unto him, and bless his name.
For the Lord is good; his mercy is everlasting; and his truth endureth to all generations.

Ainsworth's problem certainly was not ignorance; he was one of the most accomplished biblical scholars of his day. Nor was it ineptitude with the English language, for he proved himself to be an able writer of prose. The reason for his clumsiness with his mother tongue in translating the Psalms can be traced to the Puritan insistence on literal renderings. Indeed, as is stated by the translators in the Preface of *The Bay Psalm Book,* many pious folk questioned the propriety of singing the Psalms in any language but the Hebrew. Manifestly, this stance was not a tenable one, but the strictest attention was given to maintaining as close an adherence as possible to the original. This obsession, combined with the need for rhyme and meter to fit the music of the time, shackled the imagination of the translator and made inevitable the production of clumsy, unidiomatic, and wooden renderings.

It must be noted that only a few persons in early colonial communities owned Psalmbooks. In Plymouth, Brewster had one (Ainsworth's); very likely Bradford did also, but there is no proof. However, over the years the Psalms would be heard so often that an attentive person would soon know many of them by heart, for the practice was to sing through the entire Psalter over a period of time, start again at the beginning and go through them again, and repeat the procedure year after year. The person aspiring to poetry would imitate these models automatically, just as in writing prose he would unthinkingly imitate that of the Bible. Hence Bradford, once he had decided to write poetry, would naturally follow the examples that he most admired and was most familiar with.

Thus the reader should not be surprised when he reads in Bradford's poems lines like these, which are found in the part of "Some observations...," that exist in his own hand and that have not suffered from careless handling by a copyist. The lines refer to the growth of New England:

> To the north, or south, or which way you'll wind,
> Churches now are spread, and you'll pasture find.
> Many men of worth, for learning and great fame,
> Grave and godly, in to these parts here came:
> As HOOKER, COTTON, DAMFORD [Davenport], and the rest,
> Whose names are precious and elsewhere express'd;
> And many amongst these, you might soon find,
> Who (in some things) left not their like behind.[13]

In these lines, as in translations of the psalms by Ainsworth in particular, there is a straining at any cost for meter and rhythm — though both differ in pattern from Ainsworth's — and there is consistently the same failure to attain either. The difference is that the translators were constrained by the demand for literalism while Bradford was writing original poetry in which no such demand existed. An unescapable conclusion is that Bradford only partly understood meter, if at all; for he seemed to be counting syllables, ten to a line, rather than following an iambic or other pattern. As for rhyme, Bradford understood it all too well and did anything to achieve it; and he justly referred to his poems in his will not as beautiful but as "usefull." Like the numerous New England Puritans who dabbled in verse, he had a lesson to teach, a point to make, or an exhortation to deliver. The niceties of style, had he been aware of them, would surely have struck him as trivial. To him, the message of any literary work was the important thing.

IV *An Early Poem on John Robinson*

The first poem (as has been stated) to be attributed to Bradford was an elegy on John Robinson that was included by Nathaniel Morton in "A Briefe Eclesiasticall History of the Church of Christ Att Plymouth" which forms the first part of the *Plymouth Church Records* and is transcribed from Bradford's *Of Plimmoth Plantation*. Morton inserted the six quatrains of which the elegy consists under the year 1626, and he placed the work after the letter — included in both *Of Plimmoth Plantation* and the "Eclesiasticall History" — in which the governor was informed of the old pastor's death. Morton did not specify that the poem was written by Bradford (and there is no assurance that it was), but he described it as being "made by a frind on the deplored death of mr. John Robinson...."[14] Since Morton elsewhere carefully names Bradford, his uncle, as author of what he is copying into the record, it is odd that he did not do so in the case of this poem if Bradford actually was the author of it. It must be recalled that Morton compiled his portion of the *Plymouth Church Records* in the year 1680 or shortly before; and the poem, which treats Robinson's death as a recent occurrence, must have been written more than fifty years earlier. If it had been in Bradford's handwriting, Morton would have recognized it and, one would think, would have named him as the author. Perhaps he did not recognize the writing and thus attributed the verses to "a frind," either in Plymouth (Allerton, Brewster, or Winslow) or in Holland. There would seem to be no definite proof of Bradford's authorship.

At any rate, the undistinguished poem is neither better nor worse than Bradford's average. Written in "common" meter, the second and fourth lines of each quatrain rhyme. After stating that "Blessed Robinson hath Run his Race" and now resides with Christ in heaven, the poem praises him as a "shining Light" on earth, one of God's "blessed Instruments,"[15] sent to guide the elect along the paths of salvation. As in all Puritan poetry, biblical language and allusion are evident.

V *Impulse behind Bradford's Later Poetry*

The question of the authorship of the poem about Robinson is of some interest because if Bradford did write it, it antedates by twenty-five years any other verse definitely known to have been composed by him and would indicate, therefore, that versifying was not a preoccupation solely of his old age and of the period after he had ceased writing *Of Plimmoth Plantation.* Terminating his annals with the year 1646, Bradford did not complete his entry for that year until 1650, when he also drew up his list of *Mayflower* passengers and their progeny. Though he had headings for the years 1647 and 1648, he never got around to writing about them. As previously stated, the cessation of work on *Of Plimmoth Plantation* has been taken by many to be the result of Bradford's discouragement, if not his disillusionment, with the whole colonizing venture.

Although Bradford was manifestly deeply disturbed by the changes taking place in the religious, political, and economic life of Plymouth, the fact remains that he did not in any sense succumb to melancholia. He continued as governor to the day of his death, he managed and improved his own rather large (for Plymouth) commercial and farming interests, and he did not desist from writing. He did neglect his *History,* but he launched instead into two other types of composition — theological dialogues and didactic poetry — in which he had little or no previous practice. The intellectual vigor suggested by this radical change in the character of Bradford's writing does not confirm the theory that he was despondent — a state of mind totally at variance with the character of a man whose tenacity, singleness of purpose, and faith in God had carried him through far worse circumstances than those of Plymouth in the middle of the seventeenth century.

The explanation for Bradford's abrupt switch from history to polemics in prose and verse may be found in that one word "usefull" with which he described his poems in his will. though the *History* included considerable religious commentary, its main purpose was not exhortation; and, whatever Bradford's hopes may have been as to its eventual publication, it would not have served any immediate purpose. A recognition that the declining state of the colony called for something more directly exhortatory than *Of Plimmoth Plantation* may have prompted the writing of the three *Dialogues* and the six poems composed in the last years of his life. The intent of the dialogues, which have already been discussed, was clearly didactic; and they are addressed to the young men of the colony who had perhaps shown indications of backsliding. It has been suggested that the Cambridge (Massachusetts) Synod of 1646 to 1648, which issued a platform setting forth Congregational principles that were especially opposed to Presbyterianism, might have been a strong stimulus in turning Bradford to exhortatory and theological writing.[16] In the summer of 1647 Bradford himself attended the Cambridge Synod as a representative of Plymouth.

VI   *"On the Various Heresies..."*

The later poems may be considered in the order in which they appear in the Willett manuscript, where they are in the chronological sequence in which they came from their author's pen — at least as this sequence has been conjectured by Michael G. Runyan in his doctoral dissertation dealing with Bradford's verse. It should be repeated that Willett was a careless copyist — what fifteen-year-old boy set such a task would not be careless? — and that the accuracy for the text of those poems for which the copybook is the only source is not to be relied upon. At best such poems are only a fair approximation to what Bradford actually wrote.

The first poem, thus far never printed and found only in the Willett manuscript, is a lengthy piece of 1,668 lines about a number of heresies among the reformed sects, and it concludes with a plea to the Presbyterians to reconcile their differences with the Congregationalists. As the first page of this poem is missing in the copybook, the title assigned it by Harold S. Jantz will be used: "On the various heresies in Old and New England and on the Congregational Way."[17] Runyan, guided by the poem's mention, or failure to mention, certain events in the Cromwellian wars, has convincingly established 1650 as the date of its composition. Bradford's authorship — sometimes questioned — can be plausibly upheld because of its presence in a manuscript containing other poems that are his beyond reasonable doubt. Runyan has also argued for the strong possibility of an influence on this poem from a book by

Ephraim Pagitt titled *Hersiography,* published in England in 1646.
The likelihood of this influence is enhanced by the fact that at least
one of the heresies attacked by Bradford — Quakerism — was
absent from New England until 1656, though the reputation of the
Quakers would have spread from England, where they were active
as early as 1650. Pagitt, however, discusses them at some length
and in much the same terms as those employed by Bradford.[18]

This long poem, aside from its literary crudities, is perhaps the
most interesting one that Bradford ever wrote. The heresies he
describes are numerous and are denounced with gusto, and the
heretics themselves are described as idiots and sexual libertines. A
fair sample of how he deals with extremist groups is the invective he
hurls against the Ranters, a sect that believed that the Holy Ghost
dwelt within them and who engaged in noisy and disruptive demon-
strations. These Bradford considers to be the spawn of the devil,
comparing them to the Adamites, or nudists — another sect of the
times — but finding them even more disruptive of the public peace.
They are mindless, enslaved with lust, more degraded than dogs
and hogs. A disgrace to the human race, they are worse even than
any of the brutes.[19]

Among the other heretical sects that Bradford condemns are the
Familists, the Seekers, the Diggers, the Levelers, the Anabaptists —
all of them manifestations of what might be termed the countercul-
ture of the day. Other more intellectual and sedate groups and
bodies of opinion, such as the Arminians, Aryans, and Jesuits, also
receive severe criticism. As in his third *Dialogue,* Bradford is easiest
on the Presbyterians, for he recognizes that their differences with
the Congregationalists are more organizational than doctrinal. The
Presbyterian polity, with its classes (or presbyteries), synods, and
general assembly, constituted a hierarchy quite at odds with the
Congregational way and with what the Congregationalists thought
the Scriptures permitted and required. Nonetheless, Bradford
hoped that a spirit of compromise would prevail and that the two
churches would unite against the two common enemies —
Episcopacy and Roman Catholicism, both of which remained a
threat in England.

VII *Three Jeremiads*

The poem "On the various heresies..." deals broadly with what
its author considers dangerous deviations from the Congregational

way; and three shorter poems — "A Word to New Plymouth," "A Word to New England," and "Of Boston in New England" — touch closely upon local social and religious problems. Composed between 1655 and 1657, all three poems evince Bradford's concern with a period of growing materialism and slackening religious zeal; and, in doing so, they resort to the tone that characterized the Puritan sermons that Perry Miller describes as jeremiads — as laments for the past which are coupled with denunciations of the evils of the present and with prognostications of divine retribution unless the people mend their ways. The longest and most substantial of the three poems, "A Word to New Plymouth," is written in a meter that faintly resembles iambic tetrameter and that rhymes in couplets. It rather interestingly contains three major metaphors, two of which appeared in *Of Plimmoth Plantation*. The first stanza compares Plymouth Colony — not the church, as in the *History* — with a poor widow deserted by her children:

> O poor Plymouth, how dost thou moan,
> Thy children all are from thee gone,
> And left thou art in widow's state,
> Poor, helpless, sad, and desolate.[20]

The plight of the town is traceable, according to the poem, to the selfishness and the materialism of the inhabitants, who had been made rich — an exaggeration — by the colony:

> To make others rich thyself art poor,
> They are increased out of thy store,
> But growing rich they thee forsake
> And leave thee poor and desolate. (478)

The second metaphor is one derived from I Corinthians 3:6-9, where Paul states that he "planted, Appollos [another Christian] watered, but God gave the increase." Bradford's application of the text is that the plants of Separatism, "first bred" in England, continued to grow in the Netherlands until

> . . . them a place God did provide
> In wilderness, and did them guide
> Unto the American shore,
> Where they made way for many more.
> (479)

This metaphor leads directly to the third one, which is also used in *Of Plimmoth Plantation,* though it has become regrettably mixed in the poem with another metaphor:

> They broke the ice themselves alone,
> And so became a stepping-stone
> For all others, who in like case
> Were glad to find a resting-place. (479)

The stepping-stone analogy seems to have impressed Bradford and lingered long in his memory, for it occurs in the early part of the *History.* Since this metaphor, as used in *Of Plimmoth Plantation,* was included in Nathaniel Morton's *New Englands Memoriall* and in the *Plymouth Church Records,* one is tempted to believe that it contributed to the legend of Plymouth Rock — the literalizing of a metaphor. At any rate, in the stanza following the one just quoted, Bradford rather smugly points out that from Plymouth,

> ... as in a place secure,
> They [the Pilgrims] saw what others did endure
> By cruel wars, flowing in blood,
> Whilst they in peace and safety stood. (479)

The remainder of the poem, which altogether contains thirty-four quatrains, rather tediously and irrelevantly recounts the history of the various European conflicts of the period. Bradford emphasizes the Thirty Years' War of 1618 to 1648 and the war between England and Holland at mid-century, and he enters into detail concerning the English civil wars. Among Bradford's poems, this one is perhaps the most successful; for the first nine stanzas with their rich store of metaphor come as close to true poetry as any verse that Bradford wrote. In addition, the poem is of interest as perhaps a first, though tentative, utterance of American satisfaction at being far removed from the evils and disasters that blemish life in Europe — an early manifestation of isolationism.

Two other short poems mentioned in Bradford's will and included in the Willett manuscript are "Of Boston in New England" (forty-eight lines) and "A Word to New England" (twenty-two lines), both of which are in iambic tetrameter couplets. Dating from about 1654, they deplore the present state of affairs as contrasted with that of the past. Boston, whose foundations were laid by earnest and godly men like John Cotton and John Winthrop, has become the scene of drunkenness and worse excesses; and, most lamentable, as her wealth and prestige have increased, she has become forgetful and oppressive of the poor and weak. "Of Boston in New England" ends with a warning:

> Take heed ye doe not wrong the land,
> Lest he that hath lift you on high,
> When, as the poore to him doe cry
> Doe throw you downe from your high state,
> And make you low and desolate.[21]

"A Word to New England" similarly laments the loss of past glories. "Love, truth, good-men, mercy and grace" have been supplanted by "Fraud, drunkenness, whoredom and pride."[22] A true jeremiad, despite its brevity, the poem closes with a call for a renewal of the old spirit before it is too late to fend off God's wrath. Such direful ventings of Puritan misgivings about New England were, of course, standard themes in both poetry and prose. In fact, we find many of them even today in Robert Lowell's *Lord Weary's Castle,* for this poet deals with the past and present of New England and finds much to berate and little to commend.

VIII   *"Some observations..."*

Included in the Willett manuscript is the complete version of a poem ponderously titled "Some observations of Gods mercifull dealing with us in this wilderness, and his gracious protection over us these many years. Blessed be his name." All the lines but the first seventy-nine of the poem, which is written in iambic pentameter couplets, also exist in a manuscript in Bradford's hand. This large section was edited by Dr. Jeremy Belknap and published in 1794, along with the sections then extant of Bradford's *Letter Book,* in the *Collections of the Massachusetts Historical Society* under the title supplied by Belknap, "A Descriptive and Historical Account of New England in Verse; from a MS. of William Bradford, Governour of Plymouth Colony." A bit apologetic about the quality of Bradford's verse, Dr. Belknap introduced the poem with these words: "The following lines having some relation to the soil, the productions, and the history of the country, are now first printed on that account, and not for any poetical beauties to be discovered in them...."[23]

The entire text, under its original title, was edited by Charles Deane and printed in *The Proceedings of the Massachusetts Historical Society* in 1870. The colorless didacticism of the piece is underscored by Bradford's prefixing to it one Hebrew and two Latin quotations, which are included in Deane's edition. The Hebrew is from Psalm 46:11, though Bradford designates it as 46:12. In the King James translation, the verse reads: "The Lord of hosts is with us; the God of Jacob is our refuge. Selah."[24] The Latin quotations are *"Spes una homine nec morte reliquit"* (Hope alone does not desert man at death and *"Firma fides tur[r]is est fortissima"* (A firm faith is the strongest fortress).

Commencing with this pious tone, the poem launches into a diatribe against the Indians that is much more violent than anything about them in *Of Plimmoth Plantation;* but the author refers to the "happy peace" the English settlers had lived in "this four and thirty year" (465), thereby indicating 1654 as the date of the poem. The red men, he asserts, are motivated by lust and willfulness; and he perpetrates a wretched pun in alluding to them as "rude men." Sanctimoniously, he asserts that "It is God's goodness and only mercy, / That hath kept us from their fierce cruelty" (467).

Bradford has clearly chosen to ignore the Wampanoags' honoring of Massasoit's treaty of 1620 for thirty-four years, and he likewise forgets the helpfulness of the tribe in the first years during which the English would have starved had not the Indians befriended them and taught them how to grow the life-sustaining maize. At that time, Bradford was more disposed to regard the presence of the Indians as a benefit directly attributable to God's intervention. But he now chooses to omit in his poem the simple facts and to present the Indians as fierce, implacable enemies that only God, in His watchfulness over the safety of His elect, had been able to restrain from unspeakable atrocities. This stance, though deviating perhaps from truth, would be more effective in inducing backsliding colonists to renew their flagging faith in God.

At any rate, the ranting against the Indians in "Some observations..." and the presentation of them as utterly depraved and treacherous must have been done with a motive, and that motive could be none other than to demonstrate that the Pilgrims were under a special providence in those early days and, as will be seen, were in danger at mid-century of forfeiting that divine favor. In a sort of capsule history of the founding of the colony, he recalls that, after a period of near-starvation, during which life was

sustained by "fish and ground nuts" (468), a period of plenty
ensued when all kinds of field and garden crops as well as cows,
sheep, and goats abounded in such quantities that the settlers grew
rich selling their produce to the Puritans at Massachusetts Bay.
Bradford goes into detail quoting the price of a cow "at twenty
pounds and five" and a heifer at "ten or twelve pounds" (470). But
all these gifts were as nothing compared to the spiritual blessings
which they might indeed symbolize:

> . . . that which did 'bove all the rest excel,
> God, in his word, with us he here did dwell;
> Well ordered churches in each place there were,
> And a learn'd ministry was planted here[,]
>
> . . . .
>
> Where these natives were wont to cry and yell
> To Satan, who 'mongst them doth rule and dwell (470–71).

To round off the picture of bliss, "a prudent Magistracy here was
placed" and "both in th' Church and State there was true
amity. . ." (472).

About midway in the poem, however, Bradford, after announc-
ing that he is "loath (indeed) to change [his] theme" (473),
launches into a denunciation of recent evils that are threatening to
draw down divine wrath upon the land. The bill of complaints is
familiar: the rise and spread of heresies; the presence of "a mixt
multitude" (474) — of non-Puritans — many of whom had been
brought as servants; and the practice by greedy Englishmen — not
only the Dutch and the French — of selling guns to the Indians. In
denouncing the various undesirables in New England, Bradford
occasionally attains unwonted eloquence: ". . .God to such is a
consuming fire, / And they shall perish in his dreadful ire" (474).

Near the end of the poem, Bradford again evokes the specter of
Indian cruelty, from which only the hand of God can shield the
colonists:

> Do thou support us, (Lord,) with thine own hand;
> When we have need, be thou our succour then,
> Let us not fall into the hands of men (477).

The poem closes with a reference to the biblical account of Israel
under Joshua and the Judges. After the Israelites with the Lord's

help had conquered Canaan, "i' the next age they did degenerate" (477) under the influence of the remaining Canaanites and their false gods. Similarly, the Puritans and Pilgrims had been presented by the Lord with a New Canaan in North America, but they were now degenerating and incurring divine anger.

There is no surprise in the comparison of the New England settlers and their experiences with the Israelites and theirs, but the analogy becomes a bit strained when the Indians are equated, by implication at least, with the Canaanites as corrupting influences on the newcomers to their land. Perhaps, as Runyan suggests, the Indians may be symbolic of the evil and corruption latent in all people, even the English, and ever ready to burst forth. At any rate, Bradford made it doubly clear that the unprincipled lust for gain which prompted the English to sell arms to the Indians might ultimately result in disaster to the colonists. The evil that threatened the destruction of the English was ultimately of English origin. Bradford terminates the poem with appropriate references to Judges 2, 7, 11, 12, 14, and 15, and with a Latin epigram: *"Melius est peccatum cavere quam emendare"* (it is better to avoid sin than to correct it) (478).

IX *"Epitaphium Meum"*

Finally to be considered is "Epitaphium Meum," which was printed in Nathaniel Morton's *New Englands Memoriall* under the heading "Certain Verses left by the Honoured William Bradford Esq; Governour of the Jurisdiction of Plimouth, penned by his own hand, declaring gracious dispensation of Gods Providence towards him in the time of his Life, and his preparation and fittedness for Death."[25] The full, lengthy title of Morton's book announced that his purpose was to edify his readers both present and future, and one way that he proposed to achieve this objective was to introduce to the reader "divers of the most Eminent Instruments deceased, both of Church and Common-wealth ... in reference unto sundry Exemplary Passages of their LIVES, and the time of their DEATH." Bradford was obviously one of these "most Eminent Instruments," and the exemplary qualities of his life and character are fully illuminated by Morton. But to a Puritan — or to any devout and orthodox Christian — the manner and the state of mind in which one dies is of the utmost significance in that it indicates whether one is among the saved or the damned. What better evidence of Bradford's spiritual condition as he approached death existed than his own poem describing his thoughts about himself?

The main statement Bradford has to make is that from his youth he was aware of God's truth and enjoyed *"the Means of Grace."* He does not deny — indeed, he rather glories in — the fact that he suffered much:

> *A man of* Sorrows *I have been,*
> *And many* Changes *I have seen.*
> Wars, Wants, Peace, Plenty *have I known.* . . .

But Bradford, as usual, does not despair: *"Faint not,* poor Soul, *in God still trust, / Fear not the things thou suffer must."* He accepts his trials and burdens and remains convinced of the rightness of God's ways, for he is fully aware of the divine testings of Job and other biblical characters. At no time did Bradford lose hope for his own everlasting life, for Plymouth, for New England, or for the Protestant cause. As a Puritan he accepted suffering, misfortune, and sorrow as God's mysterious means of perfecting the soul of the elect in preparation for their final entrance into heaven. To a man like Bradford, a decline in personal or community fortunes would be an occasion not for self-pitying complaint but for searching self-examination, both on an individual and on a societal level, and for vigorous corrective measures.

Bradford ends his poem in the vein of one of the epitaphs to be found on many of the oldest gravestones in New England burying grounds — a type of primitive verse to which all of Bradford's may be appropriately and honorably compared:

> *Farewell,* dear Children, *whom I love,*
> *Your* better Father *is above:*
> *When I am gone, he can supply;*
> *To him I leave you when I dye.*
> *Fear him in* Truth, *walk in his* Wayes,
> *And he will bless you all your dayes.*
> *My dayes are spent,* Old Age *is come,*
> *My* Strength *it fails, my* Glass *near run:*
> *Now I will wait when work is done,*
> *Untill my* happy Change *shall come,*
> *When from my labours I shall rest*
> *With Christ above for to be blest.*

On many a New England tombstone the image of an empty hour-glass has been carved, and Bradford's state of mind as his glass had almost run would reassure his anxious friends and relatives that he was indeed one of the elect. Despair for himself and for the future of New England would indicate the opposite — that he was not of the elect — for despair is a deadly sin since it must arise from a *distrust* of God's ways and His decrees for mankind and the world. Bradford may have sorrowed at the seeming signs of deterioration in New England — Job himself sorrowed — but neither Bradford nor Job despaired. Rather, they renewed their trust in God; and they accepted His dispensation, however incomprehensible it might have been to mere human understanding.

CHAPTER 8

Of Plimmoth Plantation
as a Literary Work

BRADFORD'S minor prose and his poetry would receive scant notice, at least as belles-lettres, had they not come from the pen of the man who wrote *Of Plimmoth Plantation*. Their value lies in what they reveal of their author's mind and in the light they may cast on the values and ideals of early New England. Any assessment of Bradford's literary talents must be made on the basis of his *History*.

I *Early Impact of Bradford's* History

Strangely, *Of Plimmoth Plantation* — by common consent the greatest history written in colonial America — did not appear in print until 1856. The story of the vicissitudes of the manuscript — what Samuel Eliot Morison calls the "History of a History" — has been told in detail elsewhere.[1] In briefest summary, the manuscript remained in Bradford's family for three generations after his death; and it then found its way into Thomas Prince's New England Library, which was shelved in the steeple of the Old South Church. During the Revolution, it was apparently appropriated by one of the soldiers or officers of the British army that occupied Boston and eventually found its way to the Library of the Bishop of London, where it was "discovered" in 1855. A year later, the Massachusetts Historical Society published a scholarly edition of it; and in 1897, after much negotiation on the highest diplomatic levels, the manuscript was brought to Boston and deposited in the State Library.

Before its full publication in 1856, however, the manuscript had served as a major source for historians of New England, and its uses as such deserve attention. As has been observed earlier, Nathaniel Morton, who had long served as secretary of New Plymouth, published *New Englands Memoriall* (1669), in which he drew heavily from *Of Plimmoth Plantation.* Moses Coit Tyler, the first thorough historian of colonial American literature, has made note of certain closely parallel passages in the two authors' works,[2] and even a casual reader could find many more.

A considerable difference, however, exists between Morton's and Bradford's presentations of the material, for Morton emphasizes much more strongly than Bradford the providential element, as he saw it, in the history of Plymouth. Perhaps this tendency pleased and edified his contemporaries, but it is a drawback for the modern reader for whom quite enough "providences" exist in Bradford's book. Yet this use of Bradford's material and of sizable blocks of his prose amounts to a sort of publication and contributes importantly to the impact of Bradford as an interpreter of early American history.

Morton's *Memoriall,* nevertheless, was criticized by some Plymouth church members for being "too sparing and short" in its treatment of the ecclesiastical affairs of the plantation; and, as a consequence, Morton obligingly compiled "something more particularly Relateing to the Church of Plymouth."[3] This manuscript, loaned to Increase Mather, was burned in a great fire in Boston in 1676; but it was quickly replaced by another effort of Morton's, based in large part on material from *Of Plimmoth Plantation.* Morton carefully attributed this second narrative to his uncle and wrote it into the *Plymouth Church Records* in 1679–1680, where it constitutes "An introduction to the Eclesiasticall history [*sic*] of the Church of Christ att Plymouth in New England."[4]

Morton copied his uncle's first five chapters almost *in toto,* but with some verbal inaccuracies or variations. The ensuing four chapters he transcribed less completely, for much material in them did not relate to church history.[5] He also drew from other sections of Bradford's manuscript, using, for example, the entire memoir of William Brewster. Excerpts from these transcriptions were published by Ebenezer Hazard in 1792 in volume I of his *Historical Collections,* though rather strangely the authorship is attributed to Morton, who had plainly noted in the *Records* that Bradford was the author.[6]

More extensive portions of Morton's "Eclesiasticall history," including all the matter extracted from Bradford's first nine chapters and the Brewster eulogy, appeared in 1841 in Alexander Young's *Chronicles of the Pilgrim Fathers.* Young, like other scholars of the time, was aware of the existence in the past of a voluminous Bradford manuscript — to the value of which indeed most of its users had referred — but he considered it to be hopelessly lost. Yet his publication of much of Morton's copy of it was the most extensive exposure of it in print up to that time.[7]

Morton was, of course, only one of the early users of the Bradford manuscript. Increase Mather, for example, examined Book II (the annals section) and gleaned from it material for his book about the Indian wars, *A Relation of the Troubles which have hapned in New-England* (1677),[8] and somehow the Bradford manuscript escaped a fire which destroyed Mather's house and part of his library. Cotton Mather, Increase's son, later drew from *Of Plimmoth Plantation* for his treatment of Plymouth and of Bradford in *Magnalia Christi Americana.*[9] Somewhat earlier William Hubbard saw the manuscript and found it useful in writing his *General History of New England from the Discovery to MDCLXXX,* which was completed in 1680 but not printed until 1815. In the eighteenth century Thomas Prince drew heavily from *Of Plimmoth Plantation* for his *Chronological History of New England in the form of Annals* (1736), quoting or paraphrasing many long passages; and in the same century, Thomas Hutchinson quoted Bradford at length in his *History of the Colony of Massachusetts Bay* (1764–67).

Apparently any person in colonial New England who aspired to write a history of the region resorted to Bradford's manuscript. The wonder is that it was not published before its disappearance from Boston. Yet, wraithlike, it always lurked in the New England background — an unforgettable presence to those who read or wrote history.

II   Of Plimmoth Plantation *as Conscious Literary Art*

Ever since the discovery in 1855 of the long-lost manuscript of Bradford's *History* in the Bishop of London's library, its prose style has given rise to much and varied comment, and most of it has been admiring. An early commentator was an Englishman, John A. Doyle, a fellow of All Souls College, Oxford, and editor of the Facsimile Edition of the manuscript published in 1896; and Doyle's remarks on Bradford's style in the Introduction to this edition are brief but discerning. Quite appropriately he enters into a general comparison of Bradford with John Winthrop, the governor of Massachusetts Bay and the author of an extensive journal recording events in the history of that colony. In learning, experience, and sophistication, Doyle finds that the Cambridge-educated Winthrop cut a more impressive figure than did the yeoman Bradford. But Doyle does not concede to Winthrop a superiority as a judge of human nature or as a literary artist; for Winthrop, Doyle opines, lacks Bradford's "picturesque felicity in sketching an incident or a character."[10] In support of his opinion, Doyle cites Bradford's accounts of Lyford's arrival in Plymouth, Oldham's departure as he runs the gauntlet, the visit of the Dutch to Plymouth, and the first reception of Massasoit and his retinue.

Doyle further points out that Bradford, unlike Winthrop, had "a strong sense of literary responsibility which animates and controls" his writing, and that he "set forth at the outset with the clear, defined purpose of telling a story,"[11] whereas Winthrop seemed to have in mind no other purpose than that of writing a diary. Doyle, who believes that Bradford planned on the eventual printing of his manuscript, refers to an aside made by Bradford — "as will appear, if God give life to finish this history" (II, 110) — in support of this belief. Doyle finds evidence in the manuscript that Bradford had revised certain pages as he wrote.[12]

This same point — that Bradford was writing with a conscious literary intention — was elaborated upon by another Englishman, G. Cuthbert Blaxland, in *"Mayflower" Essays,* which was published also in 1896. Blaxland, as "domestic chaplain to the late Bishop of London,"[13] had been custodian of the bishop's library in which the Bradford manuscript was deposited, and he had studied the manuscript with care and pleasure. Most of his observations are acceptable, partly because he concerned himself with details so obvious that many critics would not have deigned to mention them. For example, he remarks that, although the manuscript is autobiography as well as history, Bradford "hardly ever permits himself to appear in the story except under the impersonal designation of the 'Governor.' "[14] Yet Blaxland has the perception to view this apparently superficial detail of authorial reticence as a stylistic device which is highly revelatory of Bradford's character.

Blaxland also points out that the meticulously neat physical appearance of the manuscript itself reveals the character of its author as well as his intentions in writing it. The exquisite handwriting is perfectly legible even to a modern eye, since each letter was separately and painstakingly formed, though variations exist in the size of the letters in different parts of the manuscript. But the care with which the whole was written indicated to Blaxland that it was actually a fair, or at least a semifinal, copy of an earlier version. Probably Bradford's reference in 1646 to "these scribled writings" that he began "aboute the year 1630, and so peeced up at times of leasure afterwards" (I, 14) was really to the notes from which the history was later written — or at least so Blaxland believes, and with considerable reason.

There is other evidence that supports this theory, especially as it applies to Book II. The first part of the manuscript begins with a presentation of the theological and political situation in which the Pilgrim congregation was formed and then traces the story of the group through its flight from England, its residence in Holland, its voyage to America, and its settlement in 1620/21 in Plymouth. This consecutive historical account deals with events ten to twenty years in the past; and its author consciously composed it as such in 1630, as he says, and perhaps revised it later. Beginning with the events of the final months of 1620 (Old Style), however, Bradford set down the story of Plymouth Plantation in the form of annals. But, since he had written nothing before 1630, the first ten annals at least must have been compiled from memory and from records in a more or less continuous literary effort.

Yet in the midst of the first annal, that for the year 1620/21, Bradford, in writing of the treaty with Massasoit, states that it had "continued this ·24· years" (I, 201). Thus this annal was either written or revised in 1644, and we may conclude that most, if not all, of the manuscript as it now exists was written or rewritten long after the events that it records. As Blaxland has put it, "We are justified, therefore, in regarding the history as the work of Bradford's later years, written in the maturity of his judgment, and in view of the issue to which the events were tending."[15]

III   *Prose Style: Biblical and Folk Elements*

Proceeding to a consideration of Bradford's prose style, Blaxland indicates how profoundly it has been influenced by the Bible, mainly the Geneva translation, though at times Bradford quotes from the Authorized Version. But the styles of the two translations are far from totally dissimilar, for each is characterized by concrete Anglo-Saxon diction and by a balanced rhythmical sentence structure. Indeed, only a very few pages in *Of Plimmoth Plantation* do not contain either paraphrases or quotations from the Scriptures, and these blend so well with the general style of the book that they often pass unnoticed, except, of course, when Bradford cites chapter and verse, as he frequently does. The result is a highly readable, unobtrusively sonorous and rhythmical prose that has often been compared to that of John Bunyan's *The Pilgrim's Progress* (1678–1684) (which was written from much the same religious point of view as was *Of Plimmoth Plantation*). It is interesting to note that Bradford's quotations from the Old Testament outnumber those from the New Testament by five to two, perhaps because he saw a closer resemblance between the story of the ancient Jews and that of the Pilgrims than he did to any narrative in the New Testament, but perhaps also because of the simple fact that the Old Testament is about three times longer than the New.

In keeping with the biblical flavor of Bradford's style was his penchant for the use of homely, sometimes earthy words and phrases doubtless drawn from his own experience as a Yorkshire country boy and as one whose duties and circumstances in later life brought him into close association with sailors, farmers, traders, soldiers. Such words and phrases are to be found throughout his writing, many of them in passages that have already been or will be quoted; but a glance back at the account of Oldham's doings provides examples. In describing the colony's difficulties with Oldham, who it will be recalled had been "a cheefe sticler in [a] former faction among the perticulers..." (I, 381–82), Bradford writes that he refused to obey Myles Standish's order that he stand his turn at sentry duty but "drew his knife at" the captain, and "ramped more like a furious beast then a man" and did not quiet down until "after he was clapt up a while" (I, 384–85) in jail. Returning to Plymouth the next year in defiance of his sentence of banishment, he again fell into a "madd furie," and the authorities "commited him till he was tamer, and then apointed a gard of musketers which he was to pass throw, and ever one was ordered to give him a thump on the brich, with the but end of his musket, and then [he] was conveied to the water side, wher a boat was ready to cary him away. Then they bid him goe and mende his manners" (I, 411).

This language of the common people is used unconsciously perhaps but zestfully by a writer with an appreciative ear. Not only is the diction that of the people, but so are the sentence pace and rhythms, which are not unlike those heard in remote rural and

coastal New England even to this day. Although Bradford is at his
colloquial best in describing troublemakers like Oldham, he wrote
equally racy accounts of the doings of Lyford, Thomas Morton,
and Weston. But at no time — not even in his most serious
moments — does he resort to pomposity or artificiality; therefore,
passages like the one just quoted do not contrast gratingly with the
general biblical flavor of his style — for the language of the English
Bible was not alien to that of the people.

As might be expected in writing that draws heavily from the
everyday speech of almost four centuries ago, *Of Plimmoth Plantation* contains many words with meanings now obsolete. In Bradford's account of the dealings with Oldham, "sticler" (stickler) and
"ramp" no longer carry the meanings they did for him. On the
other hand, "clapt" and "but" (butt), both colloquial in flavor,
have not changed their meanings. An interested reader can find
many instances of both sorts. A few examples of archaic expressions are *chatchpoule* (I, 31), a word of Provençal origin that
meant literally one who hunts fowls but that later meant a tax-
gatherer and, in Bradford's time, a sheriff's officer (see modern
catchpole, one who makes arrests for debt); *eftsone,* a Chaucerian
word, that meant *soon* or *soon afterwards* (I, 415); *sadd* (I, 401),
that meant not *sad* but *earnest, serious,* as in Chaucer; *marchante,*
that meant a fellow or chap (I, 384); *bear (bore) in hand,* another
Chaucerian expression, that meant *to deceive* (I, 378); *uncouth,*
also found in Chaucer, that meant *not known, unfamiliar* (I, 37);
to have a hankering mind after something, meaning *to covet*
(II, 216). The list could be greatly extended; and other examples
may be found in Blaxland's *"Mayflower" Essays* (130–33), from
which several of those cited have been taken.

Of additional interest are the seventeenth-century pronuncia-
tions reflected in Bradford's spelling, which was normally er-
ratic for his times, but sufficiently phonetic to reveal much about
the English he spoke. For example *ea,* for Bradford, was sounded
in many words as it is in the modern *great;* that is, it was frequently the equivalent of *ay* or the *a* in *wave,* and it frequently
replaced these spellings. Thus one finds *streats* for *straits; sprea*
for *spray (sea spray); reane* for *rain, deanger* for *danger.* Con-
versely, one sees *plased* for *pleased, craked* for *creaked,* and
wained for *weaned;* and *reather* for *rather* indicates an archaic pronunciation of the word. Other differences in pronunciation are indicated by *viage* for *voyage* (still found in dialect) and *farom* for

farm (perhaps an echo of Bradford's Yorkshire upbringing).

IV   *"A Plaine Stile"*

A noteworthy aspect of Bradford's prose is that it consciously eschews the complex, allusive, rhetorical, "metaphysical" style — one akin to the high style of the Middle Ages — so greatly prized in the Renaissance. Bradford, indeed, announced in a prefatory statement to *Of Plimmoth Plantation* that he would "endevor to manefest in a plaine stile" the "occasion and Indusments" that gave rise to the settling of Plymouth Plantation, "with singuler regard unto the simple trueth in all things, at least as near as my slender Judgmente can attaine the same" (I, 1). The distinction between a high and a low style had existed since long before Chaucer's time. In Renaissance England, the high, or "metaphysical," style, which reached unprecedented degrees of ornateness, complex sentence structure, intricate rhythms, and extravagant figures of speech, was exemplified in its most effective form in the sermons of John Donne and Lancelot Andrewes. Since the ornate style was associated with the aristocracy and the established church, it is not surprising that the Puritans, for their sermons, favored a style which was unadorned, simple, and direct. A group that recommended stripping the Anglican services of their embellishments could not tolerate discourses in which the language and rhetoric vied with the message for the attention of listeners. Language to the Puritan was intended to instruct and to inform — not to amuse.[16] The fact is, moreover, that the plain style, when employed by New England preachers like John Cotton, Thomas Hooker, and Urian Oakes, did prove effective, as it did in the *Journal* of Winthrop and in Bradford's *History.*

Since the age of twelve, Bradford had been exposed to Puritan sermons, presumably in the plain style, if we may judge from the extant writings of John Robinson, who was a minister to the Pilgrims from the Scrooby days through their residence in Holland. Robinson's published theological tracts and essays, all of them doubtless familiar to Bradford, are eminent examples of the plain style. Everything in Bradford's life and thinking would lead to his adopting the plain rather than the high mode of expression. It is so obvious that such would be his choice that one wonders that he bothered to state the fact in his prefatory note to *Of Plimmoth Plantation.*

The feelings of the Pilgrims about the two styles is cogently illustrated in an introduction that Deacon Robert Cushman, a member
of the Separatist Church in Leyden, wrote for a sermon, or discourse, that he had delivered during a short visit to Plymouth in
1621. Cushman had crossed the Atlantic on a business errand for
the London adventurers and, just before sailing on the return
voyage, he addressed the settlers who were gathered in the Common House. His text was "Let no man seek his own; but every man
another's wealth" (1 Cor. 10:24). His major purpose obviously was
to answer some of the colonists who had complained about having
to contribute the fruits of their labor to the common store. Deacon
Cushman was exercising the privilege that Separatists not ordained
to preach had of "prophesying," that is, of sermonizing; and he
was also deliberately employing the plain style, as he carefully
specified in his introduction to the printed version of the sermon.
In the event, he wrote, that any of his readers should consider his
manner of discoursing "too rude and unlearned for this curious
age, let them know, that to paint out the Gospel in plain and flat
English, amongst a company of plain Englishmen, (as we are,) is
the best and most profitable teaching; and we will study plainness,
not curiosity [subtlety], neither in things human nor heavenly."[17]

Despite such protestations, however, the plain style was not
entirely free of the mannerisms of the high style. The Elizabethan
age was one in which the English language was characterized by an
efflorescence, an ebullience, a power, unequaled before or since. In
this age of great English poetry and of great English prose, the
devices of balance and antithesis and parallelism, the generous use
of alliteration, simile, metaphor, and personification were traits of
all prose, high or plain; but they were much more obtrusively and
self-consciously present in the former than in the latter. Men and
women of all ranks and opinion seemingly took a joy in their language and regarded it not only as a powerful tool but as a fascinating plaything, as is evidenced by the frequent indulgence in puns
even among the devotees of the plain style. It was as if all speakers,
or at least writers, of the English language had suddenly and simul-
taneously found themselves in possession of an amazing new
instrument from which, like a conductor from his orchestra, they
could call forth an infinity of variations of sound and sense that
appealed now to one and now to another emotion, mood, or
faculty of the mind. The magic of language — so similar to the
magic of music — had been discovered and was being exploited to

the limit.

Thus certain stylistic mannerisms and rhetorical devices were part of the discourse, oral or written, formal or informal, of the age. A most useful study of Bradford's prose style and of its relationship to the literary currents and fashions of his era is E. F. Bradford's "Conscious Art in Bradford's *History of Plymouth Plantation*"[18] that was contributed to the *New England Quarterly* in 1928. The author points out that Bradford makes frequent and deliberate use of the devices of balance, antithesis, and alliteration and that he couples words of virtually the same meaning — all of which practices are typical of high style. In addition, attention is called to Bradford's habit of building his sentences to a climax by piling one clause or phrase on another in parallel structure, though he sometimes drops tension at the end.

Bradford employed such devices with calculated moderation, but his use of plain style did not stem from the fact that he was a "plain man." In origin, to be sure, he was a man of the people; but his talents, including the will and the ability to teach himself, were far from typical of his yeoman class. The rhetorical elements in Bradford's prose were common in almost all the writing of his era; and they decorate, though less obviously, his own and others' business letters, including those printed in *Of Plimmoth Plantation*. Yet in his *History* — it must be emphasized — Bradford was striving deliberately for literary effect; and he at times heightened his style and at others muted it as suited his purposes. Indeed, it has been suggested that he was consciously imitating the euphuistic style of Lord Berners's *The Golden Book of the Emperor Marcus Aurelius* (1535).[19]

V *Figures of Speech*

In a famous, emotion-charged passage that appears at the end of Chapter 9 of the *History* (I, 155–58), Bradford, meditating on the hardships of the ocean crossing and on the bleakness of Cape Cod in November, speaks of the "sea of troubles" that the voyagers had also traversed — a pun in its context and also a metaphor. A true Renaissance man, along with his Puritanism, Bradford had a liking for puns and used them elsewhere, as for example when he refers to Thomas Morton's "idle or Idoll May-polle" (II, 49) at Merry Mount, around which Morton's men and their Indian women companions danced and frisked "like so many fairies, or furies rather" (II, 48).

The latter pun is actually a double simile, and Bradford frequently ornaments his prose with similes as well as with metaphors. He alludes to Morton's house at Merry Mount as a "nest" (II, 74); and a few sentences later, when referring to Morton's return from England to the same house, he states that the Pilgrims demolished it "that it might be no longer a roost for shuch unclaine birds to nestle in" (II, 76). Though Morton seems to have inspired Bradford to unusual flights of rhetoric, *Of Plimmoth Plantation* is abundantly stocked with figures of speech freighted with profounder emotion than the scorn directed against the Merry Mounters.

Thus, in his description of the Pilgrims' destitution in Holland, Bradford employs personification coupled with simile: "Yet it was not longe before they saw the grimme and grisly face of povertie coming upon them like an armed man; with whom they must bukle, and incounter, and from whom they could not flye; but they were armed with faith, and patience against him, and all his encounters; and ... they prevailed, and got the victorie" (I, 37). This personification of poverty as a warrior with whom a desperate battle must be fought, with victory assured because the "saints" are armed with faith — a metaphor with biblical parallels — constitutes one of those elaborate figurative combinings known as conceits, which were so common in Renaissance literature. It is noteworthy that in this passage Bradford draws not only from his own imagination but also from the Bible — itself so rich in figurative language.

Another such oblique biblical allusion occurs when Bradford describes the misgivings of some of the Leyden congregation about migrating to North America without the king's seal on their patent. Calling to mind the parable of the two men who built their respective houses on rock and on earth (Luke 6:48, 49), Bradford writes that the overly cautious souls in the congregation feared that to go on with the American venture in the absence of full royal ratification "might prove dangerous, and but a sandie foundation" (I, 69). Such passages do much to make *Of Plimmoth Plantation* more than a mere record of events, for the effective use of them results in a stimulation of the reader's imagination to produce an effect analogous to that of poetry. Raw facts, events, and characters passed through the alembic of the creative imagination become literature or art.

But, as a historian, Bradford had to subject his materials not only to the transforming processes of the imagination but also to thoughtful analysis. His joining of these two functions has produced some impressive results. A frequently quoted example, involving the use of analogy, is in one of his speculations about the causes of the outbreak of immorality in Plymouth Colony in 1642. "It may be . . . as it is with waters when their streames are stopped or dammed up, when they gett passage they flow with more violence, and make more noys and disturbance, then when they are suffered to rune quietly in their owne chanels. So wikednes being here more stopped by strict laws, and the same mɔre nerly looked unto, so as it cannot rune in a comone road of liberty as it would, and is inclined, it searches every wher, and at last breaks out wher it getts vente" (II, 309).

Perceptive analysis, coupled with the exercise of the imagination as in this passage, conveys to the reader of this statement a vivid sense of just what was happening and of how serious the situation was. The visual and aural image of the rushing, turbulent water as it bursts through a barrier arouses in the reader an emotional reaction that is presumably akin to that felt by the responsible magistrates and church members of Plymouth as the pent-up urges of many of the inhabitants broke through social and religious restraints. The effect is similar, in fact, to that produced by the extended similes, or analogies, of Homer and Virgil.

The use of rhetorical devices of all sorts that was apparently second nature to Bradford when he wrote *Of Plimmoth Plantation* indicates his familiarity with the literary fashions of his day, especially those of polemical literature, which, even when it affected the plain style, abounded in figures of speech of greater or lesser complexity. A final example of Bradford's fondness for rhetorical embellishment is another excerpt from his speculations as to the apparent breakdown in morality; and this passage immediately follows the one just quoted:

A third reason may be, hear (as I am verily perswaded) is not more evills in this kind, nor nothing nere so many by proportion, as in other places; but they are here more discoverd and seen. . . . Besides, here the people are but few in comparison of other places, which are full and populous, and lye hid, as it were, in a wood or thickett, and many horrible evills by that means are never seen nor knowne; whereas hear, they are, as it were, brought into the light, and set in the plaine feeld, or rather on a hill, made conspicuous to the veiw of all. (II, 309–10)

Professional historians of the present century might well frown on Bradford's employment of his very active imagination in presenting and interpreting the history of Plymouth Plantation — a method that he adhered to without inhibitions. For the reader, the result is a view of history as lived and felt by Bradford, whose personality and penetrating mind are everywhere present, despite his policy of hardly ever using his name[20] and his avoiding all treatment, even mention, of personal affairs.

VI *Humor*

One of the most delightful tokens of Bradford's personal presence in *Of Plimmoth Plantation* is the humor that now and then appears. Bradford's humor is dry, gently ironic, often marked by understatement — and is not dissimilar to the traditional Yankee humor of later centuries. The lowest-keyed category of his humor consists of laconic remarks, usually at the end of a paragraph, that concern the material just presented. Chapter I describes the Church covenant that the Scrooby Separatists entered into: "whatsoever it should cost them." Bradford then adds: "And that it cost them something this ensewing historie will declare" (I, 22). The "something" was merely their homes, their property, and in many cases their lives.

Already quoted (p. 778) is Bradford's ironic comment about the value of the Archbishop's blessing on the apostate Blackwell and his company, most of whom perished en route to Virginia. Similarly, in discussing a certain Mr. Dermer, an earlier voyager to New England who had supposedly made peace with the Indians, Bradford comments, "but what a peace it was may appear by what befell him and his men" (I, 206). The fact was that Dermer and his men were attacked and taken prisoner by the Indians, and later, on Martha's Vineyard, Dermer was himself wounded in another Indian attack that cost the lives of all but one of his company.

It might be argued that some of the comments quoted above are not really humorous. Certainly they are not designed to provoke gales of laughter; but, with most readers, as with Bradford himself as he wrote them, a wry smile cannot in some cases be repressed as they read the comment. In other instances, one reacts later, after becoming aware of the events that Bradford anticipated with such laconic understatements.

Frequently, Bradford's remarks are in a much lighter and more obvious vein of humor. Such are his observations on several of the complaints that were made against conditions in Plymouth by a number of dissatisfied "perticulers" who had returned to England. For example, Bradford's rejoinder to the sixth complaint, which was that the water in New England was "not wholsome," was: "If they mean, not so wholsome as the goode beere and wine in London, . . . we will not dispute with them; but els, for water, it is as good as any in the world, (for ought we knowe,) and it is wholsome enough to us that can be contente therwith" (I, 363–64). The twelfth complaint, leveled against the abundance of mosquitoes, called forth a light-hearted sarcasm: "They [the settlers] are too delicate and unfitte to begine new-plantations and collonies, that cannot enduer the biting of a muskeeto; we would wish shuch to keepe at home till at least they be muskeeto proofe" (I, 367).

In his delineation of character, Bradford could also bring to bear a real sense of the comic. His description, already discussed, of Lyford's first appearance against the backdrop of the straggling little village of huts on the edge of the forest displays a strong relish for the absurd. Almost equally brilliant as comedy is the figure of Lyford's coconspirator, John Oldham, whose "ramping" and bellowing on the streets of Plymouth and whose second dismissal from Plymouth through a gauntlet of soldiers thumping him "on the brich" (I, 411) with their musket butts are scenes of comedy that bring to mind *The Pickwick Papers*.

Less hilarious but still amusing both to the reader and, clearly, to Bradford is the visit to Plymouth of the Dutch Secretary (second in command to the governor) of New Amsterdam. The pomposity of the secretary had been demonstrated by the incredibly flowery letter he had previously sent — the salutation of which required the equivalent of a fair-sized paragraph, "it being their maner," Bradford duly explains, "to be full of complementall titles" (II, 20). In making his visit, Secretary de Rasiere traveled by boat to Manomet, at the head of Buzzard's Bay twenty miles south of Plymouth, where the Pilgrims maintained a trading post. After reading the Dutch dignitary's letter, one is not surprised that, on landing at this cabin buried in the wilderness, he was "accompanied with a noyse of trumpeters, and some other attendants; and desired that they would send a boat for him, for he could not travill so farr over land" (II, 41–42). Bradford is good-naturedly scornful about the airs of the Dutch, especially of de Rasiere's; but Plymouth indulged on occasion in fanfare of a similar sort, as for example in its greeting Chief Massasoit on his first visit to Plymouth.

Bradford's sense of humor, so evident in *Of Plimmoth Planta-tion,* doubtless was an asset in the vicissitudes of his life as gover-nor of a wilderness outpost with its full share of malcontents and potential rebels against his authority. He and his assistants were capable of quick, strong, decisive and quite humorless actions, as is demonstrated in their dealings with Lyford, Thomas Morton, and any Indians who showed signs of opposing the English occupation of their territory. But on at least one less critical occasion their touch was lighter. This involved the insistence of certain Anglicans in the colony on celebrating Christmas in the traditional English manner. The Separatists, who considered Christmas a popish and pagan abomination, worked that day as hard as on any other. But the

Gov[erno]r tould [the Nonseparatists] that if they made it mater of con-science, he would spare them till they were better informed. So he led-away the rest and left them; but when they came home at noone from their worke, he found them in the streete at play, openly; some pitching the barr, and some at stoole-ball, and shuch like sports. So he went to them, and tooke away their implements, and tould them that it was against his conscience, that they should play and others worke. If they made the keep-ing of it mater of devotion, let them kepe their houses, but ther should be no gameing or revelling in the streets. Since which time nothing hath been atempted that way, at least openly. (I, 245–46)

Thus by deftly turning their own argument against the Anglicans, Bradford was able to avoid seeming to play the role of a tyrant; and, at the same time, he assuaged the resentment that the workers must have felt at the spectacle of large numbers of their fellow col-onists at play. Under the communal system, which obtained at this time (1621), such resentment would inevitably have been generated.

VII *History as Literature*

Such literary qualities make *Of Plimmoth Plantation* more read-able than any other early New England history of comparable magnitude and purpose. Beyond a doubt Bradford was consciously striving for literary effect, even though he might have denied that he was doing so. And it is unquestionable that his efforts, no matter how intentionally or unintentionally exerted, made his book pleasant to read. David Levin in *In Defense of Historical Literature*

(1967) has explored the relationship of literary merit to the effectiveness of historical writing. Literary merit alone, he concludes, cannot redeem an inaccurate or otherwise deficient work of history, but it can do much to enhance a piece of historical writing that is basically sound. When Levin lists a number of points of view from which literarily effective history may be judged, he finds that the most important among these characteristics are the historian's handling of time relationships, his methods of characterizing individuals and groups, and his ways of emphasizing or focusing upon these events that he considers most significant.[21] Much that pertains to these three points has already been touched upon in this study, but something can be gained by summarizing and from drawing conclusions after giving specific attention to them.

In his handling of time relationships Bradford adopted two approaches — one for each of the two books into which *Of Plimmoth Plantation* is divided. In Book I, which carries the reader up to the actual founding of Plymouth Colony, his approach is to sketch in the general historical and religious background of the Separatist movement and to single out that movement as an important phase in the Protestant struggle to reform a corrupted Church of Christ. From these broadest concerns and considerations, he quickly focuses upon the tiny church at Scrooby, Nottinghamshire, follows the flight of that congregation to Holland, briefly lingers over its vicissitudes there, becomes more circumstantial as he records its negotiations and preparations for the voyage to America, and recounts in greater detail the events of the voyage, the several weeks of exploration on Cape Cod, and finally the settling at Plymouth. In this brief and fast-moving narrative, much is perforce omitted; but Bradford's purpose is to get the Pilgrims to their New England home and to indicate at the same time how heaven seemed to favor their project in its various phases. His principle of selection was that of most writers of providential history in his time, as has already been discussed; but he does not apply this principle and belabor it as relentlessly as did most of his fellow chroniclers of New England.

In Book II, Bradford carefully announces his plan so far as chronology and selection of details are concerned: "The rest of this history (if God give me life, and opportunitie) I shall, for brevitis sake, handle by way of annalls, noteing only the heads of principall things, and passages as they fell in order of time, and may seeme to be profitable to know, or to make use of. And this may be as the

·2· Booke" (I, 187). He does present the remainder of the book in the form of annals, a common way of writing history in his day; but, relative to his speaking about brevity, he was compelled to observe it since the details of twenty-seven years of the colony's existence as known to him and as readily accessible to him as governor would have required volumes. The town and colony records during that same period of time indicate the plethora of material from which he could have drawn. In short, some principle of selection had to be applied in Book II as well as in Book I.

The principle of selection in this second section seems to have been twofold. There is the providential one on which the author relies to demonstrate the righteousness of the Pilgrims' enterprise and which constitutes the means of focusing on and emphasizing events. Equally important are emphases on human relationships as they developed from individual differences of character and from divergences of outlook and values among various groups — which emphases would correspond to two of the approaches suggested by Levin.

Enough has been said concerning Bradford's highlighting of events, situations, and enterprises in which God's involvement in the Plymouth venture was obvious to the properly pious person. It should be pointed out, however, that he was not as biased in his selection of material to be included as might have been expected. True, he omits most of the facts concerning the wrangling among the Separatists in Amsterdam and he omits all the details of the slaughter of the Indians at Wessagusset. Yet he does not gloss over the outbreaks of wickedness — buggery, adultery, fornication — in Plymouth in 1642. Thus it can be said that, though he is quite selective, he could have been more so in the direction of glorifying the Pilgrim venture and in associating it with the will of God.

Bradford's treatment of individual character has also been rather closely examined and illustrated in this study. His tendency seems to be toward caricature and ridicule in depicting persons whom he disliked, such as Lyford, Weston, Thomas Morton, and Oldham. In the case of those of whom he approves or whom he admires, like William Brewster or John Robinson, he directs the reader's attention to their estimable traits and abilities, and he omits the recording of the human weaknesses they might have had. In general, the admirable characters are members of the Separatist congregation; and in his treatment of the despicable ones, who are either unchurched or have Anglican sympathies, Bradford does attempt to be fair in his unfavorable assessments. But, in depicting both sorts of characters, Bradford does not hesitate to let his personal feelings be known; and he is eminently successful in enlisting the reader's opinion on his side — and the result is that the reader's interest in characters is high. Furthermore, Bradford escapes undue flatness in his characterization by presenting details of appearance or of manner that bring his subject to life — Lyford's cringing and weeping or Oldham's "ramping."

Inevitably, as Bradford presents either his admirable or his objectionable characters, the reader becomes aware of the contrasts between certain pairs of them: between the hypocritical Lyford and the benign Robinson; between the double-dealing Allerton and his trusting father-in-law, William Brewster; between the dependable Squanto and the conspiratorial Corbitant (the "good" and the "bad" Indians). Such contrasts doubtless existed in Bradford's mind, but he may not have deliberately arranged them for the reader. In the case of different groups of people, however, Bradford did very consciously develop contrasts. Thus in Plymouth itself there were two rather sharply divided groups — the "saints," or members of the Separatist church, and the "strangers," or Nonseparatists who were attached to the colony for economic or other reasons. Very obviously Bradford held the "saints" in much higher esteem than he did the "strangers," who were often disruptive of the peace of the colony.

There were, of course, many other contrasts. Within the company that sponsored the colony were the adventurers (the merchants who remained in London) and the planters, who endured the hardships of the New World and, according to Bradford, were misused and underappreciated by the adventurers. At Plymouth itself, in addition to the broad, inclusive grouping of "saints" and "strangers," there were those who worked for the common cause of the company; and there were the "perticulers," who worked for their own individual advantage. In contrast to the whole well-ordered, if somewhat heterogeneous, Pilgrim colony was Merry Mount with its total misrule and shocking immorality. Even the Puritans at Massachusetts Bay are contrasted unfavorably with the Separatists of Plymouth, the former being grasping and overbearing and downright unneighborly at times. Comparisons with the Dutch and the French result even more favorably for the people of Plymouth. These and other contrasts served Bradford's purpose, not only of characterizing the various groups but, more importantly for him, of demonstrating the special favor shed by heaven on the Plymouth settlers and especially on the "saints."

Whatever the contributing factors, *Of Plimmoth Plantation* stands as a literary work and as a history; the one aspect is inseparable from the other; but neither achieves the very highest rank. Although this work was too much affected by its author's religious and political views to be classed as objective history, it provides a fund of information that would otherwise be unavailable and that has been drawn upon by other historians continuously since Bradford's death. Bradford, of course, was not by profession either a literary man or a historian, but he possessed demonstrable talents and occasionally achieved immensely impressive effects. What does emerge unmistakably from the content and the style of the *History* is the character of Bradford himself, who, despite his desire to leave his private life out of his book, informs every sentence he wrote with his own rare qualities of earnestness, humor, shrewdness, and, in some instances, vindictiveness. The reader is very conscious of the varying moods and attitudes of the author — his grief and mirth, his hates and loves, his awareness of God's direction of his own and his people's lives. This was the man who was governor of tiny Plymouth Plantation — a colony the importance of which in American history far exceeds its size — during all but five of its first thirty-six years. The colony's successes and failures are traceable in large measure to him, not only as its strongest leader, but as an embodiment of its Separatist spirit and yeomanly values that underlay its founding.

CHAPTER 9

Influence and Reputation of William Bradford as an Author

WILLIAM Bradford's claims as an author rest so heavily upon *Of Plimmoth Plantation* that consideration of his literary reputation must rely almost entirely on the critical reception of that work, which has aroused such keen and continuing interest not only as a specimen of historical writing but also as a work of creative literature. Although this work's reception and evaluation as literature and as historiography are the chief concerns of this chapter, it is appropriate first to assess its influence on the mythologizing of the Pilgrims' experience.

I *The Genesis of a Myth*

The high esteem in which the manuscript of Bradford's *History* was held by writers of New England history from Nathaniel Morton through Thomas Hutchinson has been dealt with in Chapter 8. Since the manuscript was, and remains, the major source of information concerning the oldest of the New England colonies, its status and value cannot be disputed or exaggerated. Less tangible than its worth as a source book is the influence that *Of Plimmoth Plantation* exerted in establishing, in regard to the Pilgrim venture, an attitude that has persisted to our day. A myth was early created involving the settlement of Plymouth; and, rightly or wrongly, the myth has not been totally banished from the national consciousness, despite the strenuous and salutary efforts in the twentieth century of numerous debunkers or "realists" such as George Willison in his book *Saints and Strangers* (1945).

As a result, the elementary-school version of the Plymouth story, centering about the first Thanksgiving Day and drawing a romantic aura from Longfellow's wholly fictional "The Courtship of Miles Standish," has been undermined, and rightly so. We now regard the Pilgrims more as human beings who enjoyed their beer and stronger drink, who were guilty at times of greediness, who occasionally cheated one another, and who were not always kindly disposed toward the Indians. In fact, the humanized version of the settlement and early years of Plymouth is precisely the one to be found in *Of Plimmoth Plantation,* and the idealized one may be traced to such users and revisers of Bradford's manuscript as Nathaniel Morton and, especially, Cotton Mather — persons who were even more intent than Bradford on proving that the Pilgrims, along with the other Puritans, were God's people.

Bradford was of course convinced of Plymouth's and the other New England colonies' special standing with God — or at least he was convinced most of the time — though he did not permit his conviction to blind him to weaknesses among the elect, not to mention the "strangers." Yet it was Bradford who first applied the term "pilgrimes" (I, 124) to the immigrant band, and the name with all its biblical and religious connotations, as strong then as in later years, has become standard usage. Morton copied the passage including the word *"Pilgrims"* into *New Englands Memoriall*[1] and in the *Plymouth Church Records,* and Cotton Mather used it in *Magnalia Christi Americana.*

In addition, throughout New England, after the first generation of settlers, ancestor worship flourished, as it still does. In Plymouth, the centenary of the landing of the *Mayflower* was observed in 1720. From 1799 onward the phrase "Pilgrim Fathers" was in widespread use to designate the *Mayflower* passengers.[2] The fact is that the term "Pilgrims" was not inappropriate considering the religious motive that figured so largely, if not exclusively, among those of the colonists who were church members. Although Bradford had used it in passing, Cotton Mather speaks not only of "Pilgrims" but of a *"Pilgrimage,"* indicating by capitalization and italics his sense of the importance of the idea conveyed — which fits well with his treatment of the Plymouth venture as one of Christ's Great Works in America.[3] With Mather's effusion, the legend of Plymouth as a colony based solely on a spiritual foundation became firmly established in American folklore. But the seed of the legend was obviously planted by Bradford, who, as leader of a band of seekers of a New Canaan, was soon being compared to Moses, most notably so by Cotton Mather (119).

II *Early Studies and Editions of* Of Plimmoth Plantation

A noteworthy body of criticism of Bradford's *History* as a literary work emerged after its first publication in 1856 by the Massachusetts Historical Society. Indeed, interest was instantaneous and widespread, and it is not surprising that Moses Coit Tyler in his *History of American Literature: Colonial Period* (1878) not only devoted to *Of Plimmoth Plantation* considerable space and accorded it high praise, but also set the tone for much criticism that was to follow. A bit sentimentally, but accurately enough, he describes Bradford's "manliness" of character.[4] He gives condign praise to *Of Plimmoth Plantation* as an extremely useful document for historians and remarks on its author's "patristic dignity" (118). When he then describes its contents, he quotes at length and takes due notice of Bradford's efforts to relate the Plymouth colonization with the larger sweep of Reformation history. He comments flatteringly about Bradford's prose style, and he especially singles out the passage describing the Pilgrims' "condition and their emotion" (120) on reaching Cape Cod. This, he states, is "a noble specimen of simple, picturesque, and pathetic eloquence, and deserves an honorable place in the record of contemporaneous English style" (120). Tyler also calls attention to "a quaint and pithy emphasis of phrase that amounts almost to humor" in the more general "sedateness" (122) of Bradford's writing, and cites among other examples the word picture of John Lyford, which he compares to that of Dickens's Uriah Heep. But, above all, Tyler is impressed with the fact that "upon almost every page ... there is some quiet trace of the lofty motives which conducted [the Pilgrims] to their great enterprise, and of the simple heroism of their thoughts in pursuing it" (125).

The publication of a facsimile edition of the manuscript of Bradford's *Of Plimmoth Plantation* in 1896 occasioned the rather thoughtful criticism (already discussed in Chapter 8 of this study) of George C. Blaxland and John A. Doyle; and the transfer of the manuscript to Boston in 1897 released outbursts of bombast from various American political figures, all of which has been preserved in the "Commonwealth Edition" (1897). But American scholars were not idle, and in 1912 what is still the definitive edition of Bradford's *History,* that of Worthington Ford, was issued by the Massachusetts Historical Society. It was and remains a monument of painstaking and judicious scholarship, and its recent reprinting in 1968 has again made it generally available. All during the present century attention has been given to *Of Plimmoth Plantation* with increased frequency and volume in periodical articles and in books dealing with American history, literature, and religion. Only a selected few of the many useful commentaries on the *History* may, however, be given attention here.

A pioneer and still useful literary evaluation of the *History* is E. F. Bradford's essay (already noted), "Conscious Art in Bradford's *History of Plymouth Plantation"* (1928). E. F. Bradford corroborates the opinion of earlier critics, especially Doyle and Blaxland, who saw in *Of Plimmoth Plantation* a conscious literary effort, but he does so in much more detail and most notably in an analysis of Governor Bradford's style. Of certain passages he states: "The hand is the hand of Bradford, but the voice is the voice of the English Bible."[5] In addition, it will be remembered, E. F. Bradford finds in *Of Plimmoth Plantation* many of the characteristics of Elizabethan prose in general, such as antithesis, alliteration, and "the frequent combination of words similar or nearly identical in meaning" (138) — in short, many of the attributes of Euphuism, though in diluted form. Other evidences of conscious effort on Bradford's part mentioned in the article are the occurrence of similes, metaphors, personifications, and puns. The essay is not only instructive but interesting as an early analysis of Bradford's prose purely from the rhetorical point of view.

III   *Later Studies and Criticism to 1950*

Oddly enough, the *Literary History of the United States* (1946) barely alludes to *Of Plimmoth Plantation;* inaccurately describes it as a journal; adds that "none can deny the simplicity and sincerity of Bradford's literary style, nor the fact he reveals the Puritan at his best"; and rates Bradford somewhat above Governor John Winthrop in "Christian charity."[6] But other later histories of American literature have not given Bradford such short shrift. In 1949, three years after the publication of *The Literary History of the United States,* Professor Kenneth Murdock of Harvard in his *Literature and Theology in Colonial New England* gave close attention to Bradford as an author and a historian. To Murdock, as to

many others, *Of Plimmoth Plantation* is an "American classic"[7] —
a carefully planned and executed book written with the intention of
eventual publication. He points out, as have so many before and
since, that the first part of the book is an attempt to show the
importance of the experience and the accomplishments of the tiny
group of Pilgrims when they are considered in the perspective of
the eternal and bitter war between God and Satan. He discusses
Bradford's acceptance of the providential view of history and
demonstrates how this view constituted for him a principle of selection of material to be included in the work.

Murdock further relates Bradford's prose to the accepted Puritan modes in literary style, but credits him also with "an untutored
sense for a good story, a knack for the orderly knotting-up of every
thread he started to trace, and, as a special gift, rare among Puritan
writers, a vein of humor" (81). Bradford's phrasing, Murdock
notes, is not bookish but is drawn from the English spoken by his
own yeoman class — a language rich in earthy analogies and
homely maxims.

Most interestingly he observes Bradford's felicitous habit of clos-
ing his paragraphs or chapters with some pithy aphorism; and one
example that he cites occurs at the end of Chapter V of the *History*
after an account of the difficulties in obtaining a patent which the
emigrants never used: "A right emblime, it may be, of the uncertine
things of this world; that when men have toyld them selves for
them, they vanish into smoke" (81; Bradford's *History,* I, 96).
Murdock also notes the variety of tone in *Of Plimmoth Plantation*
— passages of high comedy, like that describing the arrival of
Lyford, as well as utterances in heightened prose like that referring
to the condition of the *Mayflower* passengers on first reaching
Cape Cod. Murdock's final verdict is that "no other seventeenth-
century American historian can be read today with so much pleasure, because in no other was the manner of expression so well
adapted to bring out both the dramatic quality of the story and the
author's conviction of its importance" (83).

In 1951 the first and only biography of Bradford appeared —
Bradford of Plymouth — that aims at, and quite successfully
achieves, definitiveness. The author, the late Bradford Smith, himself a descendant of the Plymouth governor, was also an able literary scholar and an accomplished writer. The accuracy of the sympathetic portrait that he presents has won the admiration of historians like Samuel Eliot Morison, and the book makes very good

reading indeed. Although Smith draws heavily from *Of Plimmoth Plantation* for his facts, his study also appraises that work critically along with Bradford's *Dialogues* and verse, to both of which Smith accords more attention than they had hitherto attracted. He quotes in full the second chapter of the *History* — the chapter dealing with the Pilgrims' flight from England to Holland. To present the account in any other way, Smith asserts, would be to deprive the reader of the pleasure of a piece of prose which "for concision, clarity of narrative, choice of the right word and beauty of rhythm ... will bear comparison with any similar piece of writing either of Bradford's age or our own."[8] Smith also considers *Of Plimmoth Plantation* to be a major American classic, "the noblest narrative of American beginnings that we have" (293).

IV   *Recent Studies and Criticism*

Samuel Eliot Morison concurs in this high estimate, as is attested by his Introduction to his edition of Bradford's *History,* which appeared in 1952. The distinction of this edition is that Morison has adopted modern English spelling, capitalization, and punctuation while otherwise adhering scrupulously to the original text. In preparing this edition, Morison worked from the manuscript itself as a final authority; he has provided copious notes and a useful and interesting Introduction that contains an amusing account of the loss and rediscovery of the manuscript. Morison's purpose, admirably fulfilled, is to make available a version of Bradford's masterpiece which, while not superseding Worthington Ford's monumental edition, is more readable for the general public. Morison, in order to attain this goal of maximum readability, has relegated to a series of appendixes many of the letters and official documents contained in *Of Plimmoth Plantation.* It is questionable whether, for a person wishing to read the entire work, the confusion caused by this arrangement is offset by any gain in narrative pace and interest. The purpose seems more laudable than the results, but each reader must form his own opinion.

Morison in his Preface writes in terms of unrestrained admiration concerning *Of Plimmoth Plantation.* The work's substance, he points out, has become a part of the national folklore, and he seems to agree with those critics who rank Bradford's prose at its best as not far below John Bunyan's or that of the King James translation of the Bible.

Normans S. Grabo in the opening essay of *Landmarks of American Writing* (1969), a compilation of critiques by various scholars, approaches *Of Plimmoth Plantation* as an early revelation of a hidden but enduring facet in American character — "a sense of moral superiority that makes ... and indeed justifies"⁹ the material success that Americans take for granted as their due. This sense of moral superiority is, of course, a natural and inevitable consequence of the Puritans' assumption that they are God's elect, who deserve the good things of this world and the next. Grabo marvels that this less than endearing self-righteousness that seems to have characterized Americans ever since the pilgrimage of 1620 — including those who assume that it is America's duty, assigned by God, to impose the American "way of life" on the peoples of Southeast Asia and elsewhere — should have been given such eloquent and timeless expression by the pen of a Yorkshire yeoman's son. Considering, however, the peculiar zeal of the Separatists, who unlike the Presbyterian Puritans permitted only "visible saints" (persons whose conduct and faith gave proof of their conversion) to church membership, it is not surprising that a leader of that sect did take for granted his group's overwhelming moral superiority.

Grabo's approach is productive and sound and quite original, for it leads to several insights and shrewd interpretations. For example, he points out that Bradford's dwelling upon the trials and sufferings of the Pilgrims, surpassing even those that beset the Apostles, only serves to emphasize how unwavering was that belief in divine favor which carried so weak a band safely through such danger and hardship. So overwhelmingly did this idea possess Bradford — Grabo avers — and so charged with emotion was it for him, that it governs his prose style and causes him to select emotion-evoking words to describe the sufferings and perils to which the Pilgrims were exposed. As a result, the Indians are represented as much more bloodthirsty than is warranted by any fact that Bradford divulges concerning them, and the plight of the sick and starving English during the first two years at Plymouth is graphically and repeatedly emphasized.

Indeed Grabo finds Bradford to be "a great sentimentalist," moved by compassion for these exiles whose sufferings derive from the fallen state of man, which even God's elect must share, despite their assurance of salvation. Yet the spectacle of these sufferings — inevitable as they are in God's plan for humanity — saddens Bradford; for, as Grabo discerns, *Of Plimmoth Plantation* "is a book of love" (13) as well as a historical document. But, as "a book of love," it does not, Grabo thinks, succumb to despair. Bradford, after all, considered the Plymouth endeavor only as a "stepping stone" — that was God's purpose for it — and he recognized that none of God's people, from the ancient Israelites to the English Separatists, had ever been exempt from suffering. The sense of their moral superiority enabled the Puritans and Separatists to accept whatever trials and tests the Lord might send — at least so they thought, and Bradford was not a dissenter on that point.

V *Historiographical Criticism*

It is difficult to differentiate between those critics who approach *Of Plimmoth Plantation* primarily as literature and those who approach it primarily as history. The fact is that any criticism would have to combine both approaches — as is obvious from the critiques just examined. However, two outstanding recent essays — one by Peter Gay and the other by David Levin — evaluate *Of Plimmoth Plantation* as exclusively as is possible from the point of view of historiography; and their views should be considered as part of the general body of criticism of Bradford's work.

Peter Gay's essay is in his very useful and perceptive volume *A Loss of Mastery: Puritan Historians in Colonial America* (1966), the second chapter of which is "William Bradford: Caesar in the Wilderness." The comparison with Caesar is itself an arresting concept since Bradford, like the Roman general, was in his less spectacular way a man of affairs who incidentally wrote history. Gay, who makes several interesting observations about *Of Plimmoth Plantation,* points out that Bradford wrote like an Englishman and a Protestant, never for a moment forgetting his origins in a nation that he, like his countrymen, considered to be under the special favor of God. Indeed, Bradford, again like most of his compatriots, strongly suspected that God was an Englishman. His *History,* therefore, and the histories written by other New England Puritans, might be taken as accountings both to God and to other Englishmen of the progress of divinely directed enterprises in the New World.

To Gay, *Of Plimmoth Plantation* is an authentic masterpiece, combining, as it does, its own special strengths with the limiting viewpoints of Puritanism. It is "in the Augustinian tradition, part of the Protestant campaign to capture the Christian past by establishing the historical credentials of the Reformation."[10] Obviously, then, to Gay, Bradford belongs to the Providential school of historians; for he wrote under the conviction that Providence was working always for the Puritans and especially for the Separatist sect of Puritans. The result, Gay concludes, is a predictable distortion of objective fact, though Bradford would never have thought of himself as anything but truthful.

For example, the portraits of Lyford and Thomas Morton of Merry Mount, Gay suggests, may well be biased. Lyford, an opponent of Separatism, was therefore evil from Bradford's standpoint. Yet most later historians have accepted Bradford's most unfavorable estimate of Lyford and do not question the part that prejudice might have played in it. Bradford's persuasiveness is the result, to a degree, of the care with which he excludes himself, except in his official capacity of governor, from the *History;* such modesty — quite likely calculated — seems to preclude the intrusion of personal opinion. Nonetheless, Gay finds *Of Plimmoth Plantation* to be "a deeply personal book" (47), not only in its concealed prejudices but more obviously in its author's sadness that was induced by the sufferings of the Plymouth colonists and by the slow but irreversible dispersal of the original congregation.

A second important historiographical critique of Bradford's *History* is embodied in a review written by David Levin[11] of Gay's *A Loss of Mastery.* In this essay Levin takes issue with Gay's view that the value of Bradford's book was limited by its author's piety and by the biases resulting from this piety. Levin's stimulating review was later incorporated in a longer essay under the title "William Bradford: The Value of Puritan Historiography" in *Major Writers in Early American Literature* (1972). The main question that Levin thinks one should ask concerning Puritan historians is not "how Puritans limited their histories but what *good* it might have done a historian to be a Puritan."[12] To this question, as it regards Bradford, Levin directs his attention, and the answer is quite simple. Bradford is unsurpassed by any modern historians of Plymouth as "an interpreter of Puritan piety.... The mistake of much commentary ... is to treat Bradford only as an *example* of piety but not to stress the achievement of Bradford the historian in portraying Puritan piety" (14).

This piety, with its acceptance of the providential nature of all events, carried with it the necessity of looking at the complexities of history and examining their significance. Whether confronted by good fortune or by adversity, the Puritans assumed that God's will was at work and that they had to try to account for its perplexing manifestations. Prosperity — assuredly one of God's signs of His support of the elect — brings on its heels misfortune. Brisk and profitable trading with the Indians would seem to be an indication that God was smiling on the Pilgrims' efforts; yet it enabled the Indians to purchase firearms with which to threaten the colonists. Prosperity in farming caused the scattering of the Plymouth population in search of larger and more fertile tracts of land. God's ways are inscrutable, and Bradford's record of how the Separatists faced them and attempted to interpret them — to examine "the natural and human means through which Providential will usually works" (16) — makes *Of Plimmoth Plantation* uniquely significant. The ending of a drought or the calming of a storm are easily explained as providential acts, but God makes use of human motives and weaknesses as well as human strengths in attaining His ends, and these uses are not so easily explained. Yet Bradford made the attempt, or at least did not avoid reporting on what he could not explain. In God's direction of history in its bafflingly uneven movement toward the final establishment of His kingdom on earth, His treatment of His faithful often seemed inexplicable and contradictory. Yet this was His way; this was the pattern of all history — to visit the chosen peoples with good and ill fortune in alternation.

Thus, Levin astutely concludes, commentators like Peter Gay have made too much of Bradford's moments of sadness and pessimism when confronted with a decline in the fortunes of his beloved Plymouth, both church and community. The whole of Bradford's *History* records ups and downs in the Pilgrims' fortunes, which Bradford's piety finds possible to accept, if not always fully to explain. There is no reason to believe that in 1647, the first year for which *Of Plimmoth Plantation* contains no annal, Bradford abandoned his lifelong view of history and succumbed to hopeless pessimism. The evidence of his writing and activities during the ensuing ten years is ample evidence to the contrary — as has been fully demonstrated in the present study.

But Levin's view that Bradford was not a victim of despair is still a minority one. Robert Daly in his article "William Bradford's Vision of History" (1973), maintains that Bradford was totally committed to the Deuteronomic Formula — that God "works through history to assure the triumph of His people and the overthrow of their enemies.''[13] Thus, when in the 1640s God seemed no longer to be working for the triumph of the Separatist cause at Plymouth, Bradford desisted from writing *Of Plimmoth Plantation,* which he had intended as a public record of the Pilgrims' strides toward the founding of the New Jerusalem. Daly is convincing in his tracing of the influence on Bradford of Eusebius, Socrates Scholasticus, and John Foxe — all of whom are mentioned by Bradford and all of whom applied the Deuteronomic Formula to their eras in history. But Daly's conclusion that Bradford decided at the end that this formula did not apply to Plymouth is open to argument. Daly's essay is interesting and provocative but rather limited in its point of view.

A major article, "Art and History in Bradford's *Of Plymouth Plantation*" (1971), by Alan B. Howard, shares Levin's perceptions but surpasses in scope and depth of treatment both his review of *A Loss of Mastery* and his essay. Starting with the assumption that bad history cannot make good literature, Howard attempts to show that art and history combine in a felicitous union in *Of Plimmoth Plantation* to make it "the most important work [in American letters] of the seventeenth century.''[14] Of great value in the essay is the summary it provides in its opening pages of the various approaches — aesthetic, psychological, theological, and historiographical — that have been adopted by critics and commentators dealing with Bradford; and Howard includes several of those already mentioned in this chapter and the preceding one. Howard also announces his intention "to see Bradford's history anew, as a particular rather than a typical or representative work ... to show the intricate process by which Bradford's providential interpretation of history shaped and was shaped by his experience..., [and] to demonstrate that Bradford's artistry is an integral part of his very rich, very complex vision of history" (242).

Central to Bradford's view, Howard believes, was an acute awareness of the complex nature of human beings — their capacity for every sort of mischief as well as for pity, love, and self-sacrifice. Driven by such contradictory impulses, humanity can function and survive only under God's directing and sustaining sovereignty. *Of Plimmoth Plantation* is indeed a drama, but it is one in which "complexity, not Satan, is the real antagonist" (249). God, then, may be regarded as the protagonist. Like all mankind, the pilgrims possessed certain God-given talents and abilities, which it was their function to use to the fullest; but they must never forget that to use

them properly they must rely on God's help. It is Howard's opinion
that Bradford's prose style, as he attempts to record the confusing
array of impulses involved in human history, is "even more
remarkable for its flexibility and complexity" than for "its simplicity and vigorous directness" (261).

Finally and most recent at this writing among critiques with a historiographical focus is a lengthy piece by Jasper Rosenmeier,
"With My Owne Eyes: William Bradford's *Of Plymouth Plantation*," which forms a chapter in *Typology and Early American
Literature* (1972). Typology is that branch of biblical exegesis that
sees Old Testament events and characters as "types" — prophetic
foreshadowings and forerunners of New Testament events and per-
sonages — but in a broader sense typology has been applied to the
interpretation of later and nonbiblical history that is presented as a
fulfillment or reemergence of occurrences and persons of both the
Old and the New Testaments. Obviously *Of Plimmoth Plantation* is
a rich field for this sort of approach: the Pilgrims are "antitypes"
(equivalents) of the Israelites who are seeking the Promised Land.
In Rosenmeier's words, the Pilgrims believed "that their lives were
divine synecdoches, minute but vital parts in the great arch of grace
spanning from Abraham to the New Jerusalem,"[15] and for this city
the Pilgrims were to lay the foundation in New England. Rosenmeier cites John Robinson as predicting a great harvest of souls
about one hundred years after the settlement of New England, and
this would mark the completion of the New Jerusalem. However, in
a much briefer time the establishment of the Massachusetts Bay
Colony and the Puritan revolution in England seemed to update the
fulfillment of Robinson's prediction by more than seventy years.
Rosenmeier feels that Bradford actually experienced pangs of jealousy that Plymouth was not the scene of these great happenings,
though previously, relying on Robinson's prophecy, he had been
content to regard Plymouth as a "stepping stone." Be that as it
may, Rosenmeier's article does bring *Of Plimmoth Plantation* into
a new and revealing perspective, that of the typological interpretation of history.

Thus present trent in the criticism of Bradford's *History*, a
book that has firmly taken its place as a major classic of American
and of English-language literature, is, on the one hand, to bring to
bear upon it more and more diversified critical tools and, on the
other, to synthesize the results of these approaches — as Alan B.
Howard, for example, has done — in an attempt to present the

work in its full and integrated complexity. Both trends will and should continue, and they will doubtless produce an increasing volume of material. For the fact is that *Of Plimmoth Plantation* is an immensely rich work, the masterpiece of a mind of the utmost sensitivity, that is annexed to a personality which is remarkable for its combining of firmness and warmth and ultimately for its capacity to love both God and humanity. Through Bradford's life and his literary work was channeled much that was most admirable, innovative, and seminal in the English Renaissance and Reformation — in other words, most of what has proved most potent for better or for worse in shaping modern minds and character in the Western world.

Notes and References

See the Preface for the titles of William Bradford's *Of Plimmoth Plantation* in its various editions. In the text and notes of this study, references, unless otherwise specified, are to Worthington C. Ford's *History of Plymouth Plantation 1620–1647,* two volumes (Boston: Massachusetts Historical Society, 1912; rpt. New York: Russell and Russell, 1968), which is on occasion designated as the *History.*

Preface

1. E. S. Morgan, "Historians of Early New England," in *Reinterpretations of Early American History* (San Marino, California, 1966). p. 42.

Chapter One

1. Volume and page references are to Worthington C. Ford's edition of *Of Plimmoth Plantation* (see *supra* the headnote to Notes and References). Book I of Bradford's *History* was probably written within a short period beginning in 1630 — perhaps under the stimulus of the establishment of Congregational polity and worship in the Massachusetts Bay Colony, for the general tone is one of elation. Apparently no part of Book II — annals for the years 1620–1646 — was completed until much later. A remark in the annal for 1620 that the treaty made with the Indians that year had been in effect for twenty-four years (I, 201), allusions in annals for other years to events occurring much later (II, 128 and 393–94), and the actual dating of at least part of the annal for 1621 as being written in 1646 (I, 218–19) suggest that Book II took its present form between 1644 and 1650, quite possibly as a result of the seeming triumph of "true religion" signaled by the discomfiture of the bishops in England. (See Jasper Rosenmeier, " 'With My Owne Eyes': William Bradford's *Of Plymouth Plantation,*" in *Typology and Early American Literature,* ed. Sacvan Bercovitch [University of Massachusetts Press, 1972], pp. 84–85.) However, Bradford may very likely have had "scribled" notes for Book II long before 1644 or 1646, and these notes may actually have been the comments in his *Letter Book* (see *Supra*, pp. 99–101). The question of the dates of the composition of Bradford's *Of Plimmoth Plantation* is discussed further on pages 125–26 *supra.*

154

2. Urian Oakes, *New England Pleaded With* (Cambridge, 1673), p. 23.

3. See the headnote to the Chronology for the practice adopted in this volume for dealing with Old Style and New Style dates.

4. Cotton Mather, *Magnalia Christi Americana* (1702; rpt. New York, 1967), I, 110. The most reliable and the fullest source of details about Bradford's life is Bradford Smith, *Bradford of Plymouth* (Philadelphia, 1951).

5. Smith, p. 41.

6. *A Dialogue or the sume of a Conference between som younge men borne in New England and sundery Ancient men that came out of holland and old England,* in *Publications of the Colonial Society of Massachusetts, Collections,* XXII (1920), *Plymouth Church Records,* Part I, p. 139. This will afterwards be referred to as the first *Dialogue.*

7. Mather, I, 110.

8. Smith, p. 54.

9. Bradford's sketch of Brewster's life and his eulogy of him was written into the Plymouth Church Records by Nathaniel Morton in 1680, printed by the Colonial Society of Massachusetts in its *Publications,* XXII (1920), Part I, pp. 75–82. It was copied from the original church records by Alexander Young and included in his *Chronicles of the Pilgrim Fathers* (Boston, 1844), pp. 461–70. Part of Bradford's account is also included in Nathaniel Morton, *New-Englands Memoriall* (1669; facsimile reprint, New York, 1937), pp. 116–19.

10. According to Bradford, Brewster served the church "above ·36· years" (II, 342). Since Brewster died in April 1643, his connection with the church would carry back to at least 1607 and probably to 1606, the latter year being that usually given for the gathering of the Scrooby congregation. Since Separatists in and near Scrooby had been meeting informally either there or in neighboring parishes for several years before 1606, one may assume that Bradford's association with Brewster began approximately forty years before Brewster's death.

Chapter Two

1. Statistics vary, but historians all agree that the "strangers" far outnumbered the "saints." See Charles M. Andrews, *The Colonial Period in American History,* I (New Haven, 1934), p. 274; and George F. Willison, *Saints and Strangers* (New York, 1945), pp. 437–54, especially the statistical table on p. 454.

2. *Plymouth Church Records,* I, p. xix.

3. Ibid., p. 148.

4. Edward Winslow, *Hypocrisie Unmasked* (1646), as quoted in *History,* I, 122 n.

5. See William Haller, *Foxe's Book of Martyrs and the Elect Nation*

(London, 1963), *passim*, but especially chapters III and IV, for a discussion of the belief among sixteenth-century English Protestants that their country was designated by God to lead the Reformation.

6. Nathaniel Morton, pp. 3–4. *John Cotton in The Way of the Congregational Churches Cleared* (London, 1648) cites the first of these reasons in the same words as does Morton (see Lazar Ziff, *John Cotton on the Churches of New England* [Cambridge, Massachusetts, 1968], pp. 191–93). Either a common source was used or Morton copied Cotton.

7. Charles Andrews, p. 194, finds that thirty-five of the 101 *Mayflower* passengers (Ford, *History,* I, 145 n., gives the number as 102) were members of the Leyden church; and, according to him, the other passengers were Nonseparatists or "strangers." George Willison, pp. 129 & 454, states that forty-one were "saints," all from Leyden, and that only four of the *Mayflower* "saints" were originally from Scrooby and that only five others, four of whom were children while at Scrooby, came on later ships. The four Scrooby persons on the *Mayflower* were Bradford, Brewster, his wife, and Francis Cooke (Willison, pp. 437–39; on p. 129, Willison wrongly omits Cooke from his list).

8. *History,* I, 189 n.

9. The governors of Plymouth during Bradford's lifetime and the years in which they served are as follows: John Carver (1620–21); William Bradford (1621–32, 1635, 1637, 1639–43, 1654–57); Edward Winslow (1633, 1636, 1644); Thomas Prence (1634, 1638). See Willison, pp. 455–57, for lists of officers of Plymouth Colony.

10. For a discussion of the high priority given to internal harmony in New England towns in Colonial times see Michael Zuckerman, *Peaceable Kingdoms: New England Towns in the Eighteenth Century* (New York, 1970).

11. *The Plymouth Colony Records* (Boston, 1855–61) and *The Plymouth Town Records* (Plymouth, 1889–1903) have been published, and provide fascinating reading; and the parts of the *Colony Records* written by Bradford actually belong in the canon of his writing.

12. See George D. Langdon, Jr., *Pilgrim Colony: A History of New Plymouth* (New Haven, 1966), Chapter 7, for a detailed and clear description of representative government in Plymouth Colony.

13. *Governour Bradford's Letter Book,* in *Collections of the Massachusetts Historical Society,* 1st Series, 3 (1794; rpt. New York, 1968), p. 59. Hereafter referred to as *Letter Book.*

14. Ibid.

15. For a discussion of the possibility of Oldham's and Lyford's being in conspiracy with certain of the London adventurers see Bradford Smith, pp. 204–05. At any rate, Governor Bradford seems strongly to have suspected a conspiracy other than a private agreement between Oldham and Lyford.

16. For a sympathetic treatment of Lyford and for criticism of Brad-

ford for his manner of dealing with him — especially in intercepting his letters — see Charles M. Andrews, I, pp. 267-77. Andrews presents Bradford as a bigot who would go to any length to protect his "purified" church against Anglican practices.

17. William Hubbard, *A General History of New England from the Discovery to MDCLXXX* (1815; rpt. New York, 1968), p. 93.

18. Thomas Morton, *New English Canaan, Publications of the Prince Society,* XIV (Boston, 1883; rpt. New York, 1967), p. 263. Morton's view of Bradford and the Separatists, who had brought to an end his venture at Merry Mount, was, of course, highly unfavorable.

19. Roland E. Usher, *The Pilgrims and Their History* (New York, 1918), p. 58.

Chapter Three

1. See David Bushnell, "The Treatment of the Indians in Plymouth Colony," *New England Quarterly,* XXVI (1953), pp. 193-218.

2. Nathaniel Morton, p. 28. Charles M. Andrews, p. 274, points out that the extinction of the Indians by plague in the Plymouth area in 1617-1619 was well known in England before the Pilgrims departed. Perhaps this particular providence did not come as a complete surprise to the Plymouth settlers.

3. Samuel Eliot Morison, editor, William Bradford, *Of Plymouth Plantation* (New York, 1952), p. 80 n, and Ford, *History,* I, p. 202 n.

4. R. G. Marsden, editor, "A Letter of William Bradford and Isaac Allerton, 1623," *American Historical Review,* VIII (1903), pp. 298-99. The slaughtered Indians were not Wampanoags.

5. For a full treatment of the affair, see Charles Francis Adams, *Three Episodes of Massachusetts History* (Boston, 1892), I, pp. 45-104. Adams admits the Indians were justified but opines that in the circumstances the English had no choice but to act as they did.

6. "A Letter of William Bradford and Isaac Allerton, 1623," p. 300.

7. John Robinson, *Works,* 3 vols., ed. Robert Ashton (London, 1851), III, p. 32; quoted in *History,* I, p. 368 n.

8. Young (who reprints *Good Newes* under the title *Winslow's Relation*), p. 331; quoted in *History,* I, p. 368 n.

Chapter Four

1. *Plymouth Church Records* (see note 6, *Chapter One*), I, p. 64.

2. Nathaniel Morton, pp. 78-81.

3. *Plymouth Church Records,* I, p. xxiii.

4. Ideally, Puritan Churches, including Separatist ones, had two ordained ministers: a pastor to "exhort" and counsel his parishioners and

a "teacher" to elucidate doctrine. The Introduction to the *Plymouth Church Records* (I, pp. xxiii–xxiv) indicates that Reyner was pastor and Chauncy teacher, but Bradford (II, p. 302) and the *Plymouth Church Records* (I, p. 74) themselves — as copied from Bradford — indicate that Reyner was teacher and Chauncy pastor. Reyner, before Chauncy's arrival and after his departure, probably served in both capacities. During Chauncy's tenure, he may have served more particularly as teacher. The functions of teacher and pastor doubtless overlapped anyway.

    5. Samuel Eliot Morison, p. 33 n.

Chapter Five

    1. Perry Miller, *The New England Mind: The Seventeenth Century* (New York, 1939; rpt. Boston, 1961), p. 360.
    2. Kenneth Murdock, *Literature and Theology in Colonial New England* (Cambridge, Mass.; 1949, rpt. New York, 1963), p.67.
    3. David Levin, a review of Peter Gay, *A Loss of Mastery: Puritan Historians in Colonial America* (Berkeley, California, 1966), in *History and Theory,* VII (1968), p. 390.
    4. Robert Daly, "William Bradford's Vision of History," *American Literature*, XLIV (January 1973), p. 558.
    5. Daly, pp. 558 ff.; see also Peter Gay, *A Loss of Mastery,* Chapter I.
    6. William Haller, p. 87.
    7. Kenneth Murdock, Chapter III.
    8. George S. Hendry, *The Westminster Confession for Today* (Richmond, Virginia, 1965), p. 49. If it be objected that Bradford, during most of his life, was unacquainted with the Westminster Confession of Faith (because it did not exist) and hence that these views may not with certainty be attributed to him, one may find identical doctrines, though less precisely stated, in a treatise by the beloved Pilgrim Pastor John Robinson, *A Defence of the Doctrines Propounded by the Synod at Dort,* especially in Chapter I (*Works,* I). The Westminster Confession, in fact, was adopted by a synod of New England Congregational churches at Cambridge, Massachusetts, in 1648.
    9. *Westminster Confession of Faith for Today,* p. 49.
    10. Ibid.
    11. For example, Peter Gay, pp. 49–52; and Robert Daly, pp. 565 ff.

Chapter Six

    1. Title page of first edition (London, 1622).
    2. *A Journal of the Pilgrims at Plymouth: Mourt's Relation,* ed. Dwight B. Heath (New York, 1962), p. xiii.
    3. *Mourt's Relation,* 1st edition, sigs. A3–A3r.
    4. Ibid., sigs. B–Br.

5. Some doubt will always remain regarding the authorship of *Mourt's Relation.* Bradford's failure to designate himself as author of any part of it (if such was actually the case) in *Of Plimmoth Plantation* when he refers to "other passages of jurneys ... already published" (I, pp. 212–13) would of course be consistent with the objectivity that he was striving to achieve. On the general question of Bradford's contribution to *Mourt's Relation,* see Alexander Young, p. 115 n., and H. M. Dexter's edition of *Mourt's Relation* (Boston, 1865), p. xvii.

6. *Mourt's Relation,* 1st edition, sig. A3r.

7. *Plymouth Church Records,* I, p. 115.

8. John Winthrop, *Winthrop's Journal: History of New England, 1630–1649,* 2 vols., ed. J. K. Hosmer (1908; rpt. 1959), I, p. 93.

9. Thomas Prince, *Annals of New-England,* II, No. 3 (Boston: [1755]), p. 70–71. Bradford Smith (pp. 252–53) and George Willison (p. 348) quote from Prince (apparently) brackets and all, making the assumption that this is how it was written by Winthrop; but Winthrop made no comments about the learning of the prophesiers.

10. *Plymouth Church Records,* p. 134 ff.

11. Ed. Charles Deane, *Proceedings of the Massachusetts Historical Society,* 1st Series, XI (for 1869–1870; pub. 1871), pp. 407–64. Referred to hereafter as the third *Dialogue.*

12. See the photographic reproductions of these pages in Isidore S. Meyer, *The Hebrew Exercises of Governor William Bradford* (Plymouth, Mass., 1973), pp. 27–47.

13. Third *Dialogue,* p. 408.

14. *Letter Book,* p. 46.

15. Ibid., a letter from James Shirley and Timothy Hatherly to Bradford, pp. 70–73; and *History,* II, pp. 66–72, 78–79, 80.

16. *Letter Book,* p. 35.

17. *Collections of the Massachusetts Historical Society,* 4th Series, VI (1863), pp. 156–61. An additional letter from Bradford to Winthrop written "in the behalfe of some Indeans of Yarmoth," who were complaining about a debt owed them by a Mr. Offley (apparently of Massachusetts Bay), appears in the *Collections of the Massachusetts Historical Society,* 4th Series, II (1859), p. 119. Still another letter to Winthrop, written in Bradford's hand and signed by him and several others, deals with the problem of indentured servants who had fled, without their masters' permission, from one colony to another. It is printed in the *Mayflower Descendant,* IX (1907), pp. 1–3.

18. "A Letter of William Bradford and Isaac Allerton," p. 301.

19. Cotton Mather, *Magnalia Christi Americana,* I, p. 113.

20. Rev. D. DeSola Pool, "Hebrew Learning Among the Puritans of New England Prior to 1700," *Publications of the American Jewish Historical Society,* No. 20 (1911), p. 34.

21. See *History of the Plimoth Plantation ...,* Facsimile Edition

160   WILLIAM BRADFORD

(London, 1896), p. 12 of text; also, see Morison, p. xxvii, for dating of
this passage. Bradford Smith's assumption, p. 305, that Bradford had
some knowledge of Hebrew before 1632 is based on erroneous evidence.
See *supra*, p. 96, and note 9 for this chapter.
    22. Meyer, p. 74.

Chapter Seven

    1. "Governor William Bradford's Will and Inventory, Literally Tran-
scribed from the Original Records," by George Ernest Bowman, *Mayflower Descendant,* II (1900), p. 228.
    2. Ibid., p. 229.
    3. The spelling and form of these titles are those that appear with the
poems as printed by the Massachusetts Historical Society; information as
to the date and place of publication of each poem by this Society is given in
subsequent notes. Unless otherwise specified, in this study the quotations
from Bradford's verse are from the poems as first printed. John Willett,
the boy copyist, spelled his last name in three different ways. Two are
Williss and Willette (see *Proceedings of the Massachusetts Historical
Society,* 1st Series, XI, p. 466. The spelling Willett also occurs and is that
adopted by Ford (*History,* II, p. 421).
    4. Willison, p. 339.
    5. Michael G. Runyan, "The Poetry of William Bradford: An Anno-
tated Edition with Essays Introductory to the Poems." Ph.D. Dissertation, University of California at Los Angeles, 1970, p. 258.
    6. Miller, pp. 360–61.
    7. Quoted by Miller, p. 361.
    8. Murdock, p. 143.
    9. Ibid., p. 146, quoted from Cotton Mather, *A Faithful Man,
Described and Rewarded* (Boston, 1705), p. 24.
    10. Quoted by Miller, p. 361. See also *The Bay Psalm Book* (1640; fac-
simile rpt. Chicago, 1956), sig. **3r.
    11. H. W. Longfellow, *The Complete Poetical Works* (Boston, 1893),
p. 169.
    12. Henry Ainsworth, *Annotations on the Booke of Psalmes...,* 2nd
edition (Amsterdam, 1617). The metrical versions of the Psalms, along
with the musical notations, are in Part II of this volume, which is not pagi-
nated. Psalm 100 may be found in sigs. K3 and K3r. For a full discussion
of Ainsworth's version of the Psalms, see Waldo S. Pratt, *The Music of
the Pilgrims* (Boston, 1921).
    13. *Proceedings of the Massachusetts Historical Society,* 1st Series, XI,
pp. 471–72.
    14. *Plymouth Church Records,* I, p. 62. For authorship of poem, see
Harold S. Jantz, *The First Century of New England Verse* (1944; rpt. New
York, 1962), p. 182.

15. *Plymouth Church Records,* I, pp. 62–63.

16. Runyan, p. 43.

17. Jantz, p. 182.

18. On the question of authorship see Jantz, p. 15; *Proceedings of the Massachusetts Historical Society,* 1st Series, XI, p. 466 n.; and Runyan, pp. 40–41.

19. Runyan, pp. 52–53.

10. *Proceedings of the Massachusetts Historical Society,* 1st series, XI, p. 478.

21. *Collections of the Massachusetts Historical Society,* 3rd Series, VII (1838), p. 28.

22. Ibid.

23. *Collections of the Massachusetts Historical Society,* 1st Series, III, p. 77.

24. *Proceedings of the Massachusetts Historical Society,* 1st Series, IX, p. 465. All references to "Some observations..." are to this edition (not that of 1794) and are given in parenthesis in the text.

25. Morton, p. 144. The poem appears on pp. 144–45, where the quoted passages may be found.

Chapter Eight

1. Morison, pp. xxvii–xlii; see also introductory sections of *Bradford's History "Of Plimoth Plantation"* (Boston, 1897), the so-called Commonwealth Edition, prepared "from the original manuscript ... by order of the General Court of Massachusetts" and edited by the Secretary of the Commonwealth.

2. M. C. Tyler, *A History of American Literature During the Colonial Period, 1607-1765* (New York, 1909), p. 126 ff.

3. *Plymouth Church Records,* I, p. 5.

4. Ibid., p.6.

5. *History,* I, p. 158 n.

6. *Historical Collections; Consisting of State Papers...* (1792-94; rpt. Freeport, N.Y., 1972), I, pp. 349–73.

7. See *Plymouth Church Records,* I, p. 51 n; also *History,* I, p. 158 n.

8. Increase Mather does not specifically mention having read Book I. In his "To the Reader" he states: "...I have read a large Manuscript of Governor Bradfords (written with his own hand,) being expressive of what the *first planters* in this countrey met with, whether from the *Heathen* or otherwise, from the year 1620 to the year 1647." *A Relation of the Troubles...* (1677; rpt. New York, 1972). Increase Mather not only gleaned material from Bradford but on occasion used, without quotation marks, his phrasing and sentences, or even longer passages, almost verbatim (compare Mather's p. 55 with *History,* II, p. 263 ff, and Mather's p. 57 ff with *History,* II, pp. 370–72).

9. Morison, pp. xxvii–xxxi; *History,* II, pp. 413–15. See E. F. Bradford, "Conscious Art in Bradford's *History of Plymouth Plantation*" *New England Quarterly,* I (1928), p. 136, for evidence that Cotton Mather used Bradford's *History* while writing his *Magnalia.*

10. John A. Doyle, ed., *History of the Plimoth Plantation...* Facsimile Edition, p. 16.

11. Ibid.

12. Ibid., pp. 14–16. Some of the evidences of revision that Doyle observed might have been changes and corrections made in the manuscript by Thomas Prince while drawing from it for his *Annals of New-England.*

13. G. C. Blaxland, *"Mayflower" Essays on the Story of the Pilgrim Fathers as Told in Governor Bradford's MS. History of the Plimoth Plantation...* (London, 1896), see title page.

14. Ibid., p. 101.

15. Ibid., p. 105. See note 1, Chapter I, for the alternate theory to the effect that Book I was composed as it now stands, with little or no revision, in a short period during or right after 1630. Differences in handwriting and ink lend support to this theory.

16. Miller, Chapter XII: "The Plain Style."

17. Young, pp. 260–61. See also *History,* I, pp. 235–36 n.

18. E. F. Bradford, pp. 133–57.

19. Ibid., p. 146. See also *History,* I, p. 42 n. Indeed, in a note to the Robinson passage, William Bradford himself refers to Berners's translation of the "Goulden boke" (I, p. 42), which had inspired John Lyly's *Euphues* (1578).

20. Bradford refers to himself by name at the time he is elected governor after Carver's death (I, p. 216) and in connection with his surrender (in March 1640/41) of the Plymouth Patent, which had been granted solely to him, to the freemen of the colony. In both these instances, it will be noted, he cited his name only in relationship to highly official, or public, matters. His name, of course, does appear in documents and letters that he quotes. He uses the pronoun *I* quite frequently in his narrative or expository passages. See Blaxland, p. 109.

21. David Levin *In Defense of Historical Literature* (New York, 1967), Chapter I, "The Literary Criticism of History," p. 1–33.

Chapter Nine

1. *New Englands Memoriall,* p. 5, where the phrasing is *"Pilgrims and Strangers."* In *Plymouth Church Records,* p. 43, Morton retains Bradford's phrase, "They kne[w] they were pilgrimes."

2. Morison, p. xxxi.

3. *Magnalia Christi Americana,* I, p. 54. See also Thomas Hutchinson, *The History of the Colony and Province of Massachusetts-Bay,* ed. L. S. Mayo (Cambridge, Massachusetts, 1936), II, p. 346 n. Hutchinson,

whose *History* appeared in 1764 and 1767, states: "I think I may with singular propriety call the [Plymouth settlers'] lives a pilgrimage....
After having arrived to the meridian of life, the declining part was to be spent in another world, among savages, of whom every European must have received a most unfavourable if not formidable idea. *Tantum religio potuit suadere* [To such lengths can religion lead]." Hutchinson was well acquainted with *Of Plimmoth Plantation* in manuscript, from which he quoted extensively.

4. Tyler, p. 116.

5. E. F. Bradford, p. 135.

6. Robert E. Spiller, Willard Thorpe, et al., eds., *Literary History of the United States* (New York, 1948), I, p. 34.

7. Murdock, p. 78.

8. Smith, p. 67.

9. Norman S. Grabo, *"William Bradford: Of Plymouth Plantation,"* in *Landmarks of American Writing,* ed. Hennig Cohen (New York, 1969), pp. 3-4.

10. Peter Gay, *A Loss of Mastery: Puritan Historians in Colonial New England* (Berkeley, 1966), p. 32.

11. David Levin, Review of Peter Gay, *A Loss of Mastery...*, in *History and Theory,* VII (1968), pp. 385-93.

12. David Levin, "William Bradford: The Value of Puritan Historiography," in *Major Writers in Early American Literature,* ed. Everett Emerson (Madison, Wisconsin, 1972), p. 13.

13. Robert Daly, "William Bradford's Vision of History," *American Literature,* XLIV (1973), p. 558.

14. Alan B. Howard, "Art and History in Bradford's *Of Plymouth Plantation,*" *William and Mary Quarterly,* XXVIII (1971), p. 238.

15. Jasper Rosenmeier, " 'With My Owne Eyes': William Bradford's *Of Plymouth Plantation,*" in *Typology and Early American Literature,* ed. Sacvan Bercovitch (Amherst, 1972), p. 30.

Selected Bibliography

PRIMARY SOURCES

1. Writings of William Bradford arranged chronologically by date of first complete publication. (In several cases more scholarly or more accessible editions are given preferential citation along with that of the first printing.)

A Relation or Journal of the beginning and proceedings of the English Plantation setled at Plimoth in New England. (With Edward Winslow.) London: John Bellamie, 1622. Commonly known as *Mourt's Relation.*

"Certain Verses left by the Honoured William Bradford Esq. . . ." (otherwise known as "Epitaphium Meum"). In Nathaniel Morton, *New Englands Memoriall.* Cambridge: printed by S.G. and M.G. for John Usher of Boston, 1669, pp. 144–45.

Governour Bradford's Letter Book. [Ed. Jeremy Belknap.] *Collections of the Massachusetts Historical Society for 1794* [1st series], III Boston, n.d., 27–76.

"A Word to Boston" (two poems: "Of Boston in New England" and "A Word to New England"). *Collections of the Massachusetts Historical Society,* 3rd series, VII. Boston, 1838, 27–28.

A Dialogue or the sume of a Conference between som younge men borne in New England and sundery Ancient men that came out of holland and old England Anno dom 1648 [The first *Dialogue*]. *Publications of the Colonial Society of Massachusetts. Collections.* XXII. Boston, 1920. *Plymouth Church Records*, Part I, 115–41. First printed fully but less accurately in Alexander Young, *Chronicles of the Pilgrim Fathers.* Boston: C. C. Little and J. Brown, 1941.

History of Plymouth Plantation, 1620–1647 (Of Plimmoth Plantation). Ed Worthington C. Ford. Two Volumes. Boston: The Massachusetts Historical Society, 1912. The first complete published edition was *History of Plymouth Plantation.* Ed. Charles Deane. *Collections of the Massachusetts Historical Society,* 4th series, II. Boston, 1856.

"Letter from William Bradford to John Winthrop." *Collections of the Massachusetts Historical Society,* 4th series, II. Boston, 1859, 119.

"Letters of William Bradford." *Collections of the Massachusetts Historical Society,* 4th series, VI. Boston, 1863, 156–61.

A Dialogue Or · 3d· Conference betweene some Yonge-men borne in New-England, and some Ancient-men, which came out of Holand and Old England, concerning the Church, and the govermente therof [The third *Dialogue*]. Ed. Charles Deane. *Proceedings of the Massachusetts Historical Society,* 1st series, XI. Boston, 1871, 396–464.

"Some observations of God's merciful dealing with us in this wilderness, and his gracious protection over us these many years. Blessed be his name" and "A Word to New Plymouth." Ed. Charles Deane. *Proceedings of the Massachusetts Historical Society,* 1st series, XI. Boston: published for the Society, 1871, 465–82.

"Governor William Bradford's Will and Inventory." Literally transcribed from the original records, by George Ernest Bowman. *The Mayflower Descendant,* II (1900), 228–34.

"A Letter of William Bradford and Isaac Allerton, 1623." Ed. R. G. Marsden. *American Historical Review,* VIII (1903), 294–301.

"Governor Bradford's Letter to Governor Winthrop." Transcribed from the Original Document by George Ernest Bowman. *The Mayflower Descendant,* IX (1907), 1–3.

"[A] few poems made by a frind on the deplored death of mr. John Robinson..." (an elegy of six quatrains). *Publications of the Colonial Society of Massachusetts. Collections.* (1920). *Plymouth Church Records,* Part I, 62–63.

A Letter of William Bradford to Christopher Ellis at Leyden. In Daniel Plooij, *The Pilgrim Fathers from a Dutch Point of View.* New York: New York University Press, 1932, pp. 83–84.

2. Manuscripts

The manuscript of *Of Plimmoth Plantation* is deposited in the Massachusetts State Library. Most other manuscripts are in the possession of the Massachusetts Historical Society.

SECONDARY SOURCES

From the vast number of books and articles that have been written about the colony of New Plymouth and its founders — most of which have direct bearing on the life and work of William Bradford — the following have been selected as being exceptionally helpful. Other studies are cited in the notes.

BLAXLAND, G. CUTHBERT. *"Mayflower" Essays on the Story of the Pilgrim Fathers as told in Governor Bradford's Ms. History....* London: Ward and Downey, 1896. Early and still illuminating commentary on Bradford as man and writer.

BRADFORD, E. F. "Conscious Art in Bradford's *History of Plymouth Plantation." New England Quarterly,* I (1928), 133–57. Detailed, discerning study of Bradford's prose style.

BREWSTER, DOROTHY. *William Brewster of the Mayflower.* New York: New York University Press, 1970. Biography of Bradford's close friend and mentor.

BURGESS, WALTER. *John Robinson: Pastor of the Pilgrim Fathers.* London: Williams and Norgate, 1920. Sound presentation of the life and theological opinions of an important Separatist.

BUSHNELL, DAVID. "The Treatment of the Indians in Plymouth Colony." *New England Quarterly,* XXVI (1953), 193-218. Brief, well-documented study.

DALY, ROBERT. "William Bradford's Vision of History." *American Literature,* XLIV (1973), 557-69. Discusses *Of Plimmoth Plantation* in the context of Christian historiography.

DEXTER, HENRY M., and DEXTER, MORTON. *The England and the Holland of the Pilgrims.* Boston: Houghton, Mifflin and Company, 1905. Definitive and indispensable.

DILLON, FRANCIS. *A Place for Habitation: The Pilgrim Fathers and Their Quest.* London: Hutchinson and Company, 1973. Good recent study.

GAY, PETER. *A Loss of Mastery: Puritan Historians in Colonial America.* Berkeley: University of California Press, 1966. Considerable attention is given to Bradford in his relationship to other New England historians and in general to Puritan historiography.

GRABO, NORMAN. "William Bradford: *Of Plymouth Plantation.*" *Landmarks of American Literature.* Ed. Hennig Cohen. New York: Basic Books, 1969, pp. 3-19. Illuminating critical assessment.

HOWARD, ALAN B. "Art and History in Bradford's *Of Plymouth Plantation.*" *William and Mary Quarterly.* XXVIII (1971), 237-66. Major contribution to the study of Bradford's literary talent.

JANTZ, HAROLD. *The First Century of New England Verse.* 1st ed., 1943; rpt. New York: Russell and Russell, 1962. Places Bradford's verse in the context of its time and tradition; contains the authoritative listing of his poems (p. 182).

LANGDON, GEORGE D., JR. *Pilgrim Colony: A History of New Plymouth.* New Haven: Yale University Press, 1966. Especially strong on the political and economic life of the colony.

LEVIN, DAVID. *In Defense of Historical Literature: Essays on American History, Autobiography, Drama, and Fiction.* New York: Hill and Wang, 1967. Presents interesting set of criteria for the criticism of history as literature.

_____. "William Bradford: the Value of Puritan Historiography." *Major Writers of Early American Literature.* Ed. Everett Emerson. Madison: University of Wisconsin Press, 1972. Makes a convincing case for the acceptance of Bradford's *Of Plimmoth Plantation* in terms of its author's religious premises.

McINTYRE, RUTH. *Debts Hopeful and Desperate: Financing the Plymouth Colony.* Plymouth: Plimoth Plantation, 1963. Most helpful elucidation of the tangled finances described by Bradford in *Of Plimmoth Plantation*.

MEYER, ISIDORE S. *The Hebrew Exercises of Governor William Brad-* Plymouth: Pilgrim Society, 1973. Complete presentation and discussion of Bradford's preoccupation with the language of the Old Testament.

MILLER, PERRY. *The New England Mind: The Seventeenth Century.* 1st ed., 1939; rpt. Boston: Beacon Press, 1961. A classic.

———. *Orthodoxy in Massachusetts.* 1st ed., 1933; rpt. New York: Harper and Row, 1970. Outstanding study of New England Congregationalism.

MURDOCK, KENNETH B. *Literature and Theology in Colonial New England.* 1st ed., 1949; rpt. New York: Harper and Row, 1963. Contains an excellent general commentary on *Of Plimmoth Plantation* in the context of the literary tradition of which it was a part.

Records of the Colony of New Plymouth in New England. 12 vols. Eds. Nathaniel Shurtleff and David Pulsifer. Boston: from the Press of William White, Printer to the Commonwealth, 1855-61. Invaluable for source material; most of the records before January 1636/37 written in Bradford's hand.

ROBINSON, JOHN. *Works.* 3 vols. Ed. Robert Ashton. London: John Snow, 1851. Main source of Bradford's theological views.

ROSENMEIER, JASPER. " 'With My Owne Eyes': William Bradford's *Of Plymouth Plantation.*" *Typology and Early American Literature.* Ed. Sacvan Bercovitch. Amherst: University of Massachusetts Press, 1972. Perceptive typological interpretation of Bradford's *History*.

RUNYAN, MICHAEL G. *The Poetry of William Bradford: An Annotated Edition with Essays Introductory to the Poems.* Doctoral Dissertation. University of California at Los Angeles, 1970. Unpublished.

SMITH, BRADFORD. *Bradford of Plymouth.* Philadelphia: J. B. Lippincott Company, 1951. Best biography of Bradford. Contains useful bibliography.

WALKER, WILLISTON. *Ten New England Leaders.* New York: Silver, Burdett and Company, 1901. Presents Bradford (pp. 3-45) as prototypal Congregationalist.

WILLISON, GEORGE FINDLEY. *Saints and Strangers.* New York: Reynal and Hitchcock, 1945. Most comprehensive study yet published on all aspects of Plymouth Colony and its founders. Contains excellent bibliography.

YOUNG, ALEXANDER. *Chronicles of the Pilgrim Fathers.* Boston: C. C. Little and J. Brown, 1841. Valuable compendium of writing related to the founding of Plymouth Plantation. Contains *Mourt's Relation,* the first printing (in modernized spelling) of Bradford's first *Dialogue,* Robert Cushman's discourse at Plymouth in 1622, etc.

Index

DATE DUE

GAYLORD			PRINTED IN U.S.A.